Old Testament Prophecy

Stories of the Biblical Prophets, including Amos, Ezekiel, Jeremiah, Haggai and Zechariah

By Frank Knight Sanders

PANTIANOS
CLASSICS

Published by Pantianos Classics

ISBN-13: 978-1-78987-096-1

First published in 1921

Contents

Preface

The aim of this volume is to furnish an accurate survey of the whole prophetic material of the Old Testament and a correct foundation for religious thinking. The outlines show the historical development and the gradual upward trend of prophetic teaching to its culmination in the interpretation of religion as a missionary enterprise. The volume is entirely readable, yet it is so arranged that it may be used as a text-book for college classes, Bible classes, teacher training classes in community schools of religion and elsewhere, furnishing the essential data for profitable discussion.

The Appendix furnishes apparatus for the aid of the teacher or class leader. Every reader can test his grasp of Old Testament prophecy by answering the questions in the third section of the Appendix. For classroom discussions the suggested topics in Appendix IV will be found useful. No questions are raised that cannot reasonably be discussed by those using this book. The first four volumes of the series of which this is a part give a correct perspective for both the Old and the New Testament. Each volume, however, is complete in itself.

No one should expect that the study of so small a volume will afford a mastery of prophetic literature. This book has a less pretentious but more useful aim. It will lay a secure basis for an appreciation of the nature and value of prophecy, for its intelligent interpretation, and for its lifelong enjoyment.

The Editors.

July. 1921.

Introductory

To one who has gained a reasonable familiarity with Old Testament history the study of the prophetical literature of the Old Testament in its proper historical sequence will be a fascinating and richly rewarding task. The prophets were the real leaders of Hebrew religious thinking. Through them came the gradual shaping of that thinking into so satisfactory an interpretation of God, man, and the universe that it gained an almost universal recognition as the best constructive religious platform ever developed in the ages before Christ. It was a long and slow process over many centuries. Whoever desires to gain a working grasp of the heart of the Old Testament must acquire a comprehensive knowledge in their proper sequence of these prophetic records, found in the Old Testament books from Isaiah to Malachi, and must understand their outstanding ideas. Such a knowledge will become a reliable basis for the more intensive study of portions of the prophetic declarations, which may be necessary as a preliminary to their most effective use and to a full recognition of their exact values in supplementing and illuminating the historical Old Testament records and in shaping the upward social and religious growth of the Hebrew people.

The student will quickly discover that the prophets, at least the best of them, were social reformers and statesmen quite as distinctively as preachers about God and His world. In their mind life did not exist in compartments. A truer idea of God compelled men who were loyal to Him to readjust their social and political procedure. The analogue to-day of a prophet is the fearless Christian preacher trained to have a vision of what must be done, if the principles and spirit of our Lord are to regulate the life of to-day. The prophet spoke for God to man, interpreting His will. He was designated variously as a "seer" (I Samuel 9: 9), a "man of God" (I Kings 17: 18), as a "servant" of God (Isaiah 20: 3), as an "interpreter" (Isaiah 43: 27, *margin*) or as a "watchman" (Ezekiel 3: 17).

A true prophet was always far in advance of his age, otherwise he could not have been a religious discoverer. He was a man of holy visions, whose eyes were fixed upon an unrealized future, yet, like Columbus, he equipped a good, stout ship in which to make the venture. The prophet was also a man of his own generation, interested primarily in its reformation and inspiration to loftier service, holding up the ideal future as something which served as an understandable goal. The more these great leaders and their writings are studied, the less do they appear as men who existed for the mere purpose of declaring something in God's name about a future which was beyond the human experience of the prophet's age, although the prediction of an assured religious future was very generally one of the methods which they used for impressing upon their constituencies a definite present obligation of duty. This task of prediction was auxiliary to their predominating task of making their people more righteous, more obedient, more responsive to God, more conscious of His real nature and of His place in their affairs. It helped to magnify God's power and purpose and to impress men's minds with the continuity of His plans for the world. It is their intensively earnest emphasis upon every-day religion and morality which makes their writings helpful and stimulating for every age.

No one can gain a right impression of these remarkable leaders of religious thinking, or of their contributions, unless the prophetic records are readjusted into a proper sequence for study. The prophetic writings, major and minor, as we find them in the English Bible, are not arranged in their true chronological order. Isaiah is probably the third in order instead of being the first; Jeremiah the sixth instead of the second; Amos the first, not the seventh. Malachi is by no means the latest of the group. No one knows to-day on what principle these writings were arranged by the scribal editors of the second or third century before Christ, but unquestionably it was not the principle of historical sequence. In the following studies the process of establishing a specific sequence involves many minor decisions, regarding which some students of prophecy may differ from the editors, yet the order adopted represents the general conclusions on which students who are not extreme in opinion are fairly agreed. No student of Old Testament prophecy can doubt that such books as Isaiah, Micah, Jeremiah, and Zechariah show clearly that they include material related to the thinking and experience of more than one generation. Such differing sections of the respective books are studied below in connection with the age to which they carried a message. Since this series of studies is general in aim rather than intensive, the minor intricacies of critical judgment are ignored, lest they should prove merely confusing. These studies do not take the place of a first-rate commentary or textbook, but hope to serve as an illuminating introduction to a later, closely detailed, exacting but fruitful study of any particular prophetic utterance or period.

A consideration of the uniqueness of Hebrew prophecy is reserved until the closing chapter, after the data are all in hand. It may be helpful to call attention at the outset to the undeniable fact that the Hebrew prophetic order grew out of conditions very definitely paralleled in other nations of the same class and period. All early religions had some method of getting at the will of the gods, partly by the various methods of necromancy, partly through the supposedly inspired utterances or conclusions of those who could throw themselves into a state of ecstasy or trance. We have no means of judging the methods employed by Miriam (Exodus 15: 20), Balaam (Numbers 22-24), or even Deborah (Judges 4:4). In the last case, as well as in that of Abraham

(Genesis 20: 7), the prophetical task is not made perfectly clear by the context. Perhaps Abraham, like Moses (Deuteronomy 34: 10), was so known to posterity because each had to do with the beginnings of a Hebrew religious consciousness. One who traces the history of the development of the prophetic order among the Hebrews reaches firm ground in the days of Samuel. That leader was recognized by the Hebrew people as one through whom Jehovah could communicate His will (I Samuel 3: 20). Samuel had a personality of transforming power. Under his leadership groups of young men who may have been religious enthusiasts or merely patriotic in purpose were gradually organized (I Samuel 9:5-10: 13; 19: 18-24) into a sort of brotherhood and brought under some sort of control. Other leaders developed, such as Gad (I Samuel 22: 5). Soothsayers still existed (I Samuel 28: 6-25), who were consulted by the people, but when men of such evident strength and sanity as Nathan and Gad were both the leaders of such a brotherhood and devoted counsellors of David (II Samuel 7:1-17; 12:1-15; 24:11-14; I Kings 1: 8-40), they rapidly attained great influence throughout the kingdom. Under such sane, dignified leadership as they could give it is easy to understand how the prophetic body developed, in the course of a century or so, into an order of considerable size and of much social influence (I Kings 18: 4). In the days of Ahab its great representatives were fearless counsellors (I Kings 20: 13-15, 35-43) and keen critics (I Kings 21:17-26; 22:5-28) in matters of great import. On the other hand, hundreds of members of the prophetic order were easy-going sycophants (I Kings 22: 6). The prophet Micaiah told Ahab to his face that many of those who thronged his court were deliberate liars (I Kings 22: 23); while the prophet Micah drew a keen contrast between all such falsely termed prophets, to whom their position was a mere means of an easy livelihood, and a real speaker for God (Micah 3: 5-8).

Elijah and Elisha were each remarkable men. The former was the more of a leader. He had wonderful courage. Almost single-handed he stood for righteousness and for national loyalty to Jehovah. Elisha was better fitted to carry the program through. He was closer to the hearts of the people. Such prophets made the order great.

Whatever the actual course of the development of the prophetic order, in the ninth century B. C. it had become a very real and important factor in the social and religious life of the Hebrew peoples, playing a part in friendly relations with the people not unlike that of the friars of the Middle Ages. Some of these prophets were real saints, respected and beloved as upholders of the teachings and service of Jehovah. Others, all too many of them, were corrupt, lazy, and unspiritual, becoming members of the order to gain an easy livelihood. Such a mingling of worthy and unworthy members has characterized every great movement in history. The fact that the unworthy members are so often criticized sharply by prophetic writers is a very good evidence of the general truthfulness of their records. The significant fact remains that within the general range of this professional group of social and religious advisers there developed a leadership which not only differentiated the type of its influence from that of similar groups in adjoining lands, but which also rendered to the Hebrew people and through them to the world of our day an incomparable service.

I - The First Literary Prophet - Amos The Herdsman (About 745 B. C.)

From the days of David and Solomon onward there is abundant evidence that one increasingly important public function, performed, as a rule, by members of the prophetic order, was that of historical composition. The prophets some of them, at least had the requisite leisure and education for literary tasks. Whether the official chroniclers of the cabinets of David (II Samuel 8: 16; 20: 24) and of Solomon (I Kings 4: 3) and his successors, who kept the records which are at the basis of the books of Kings (I Kings 14: 19, 29 and after), were of the prophetic order there is no sure means of determining. It is regarded as highly probable, however, that the vivid narratives of early Old Testament history which describe the days of the patriarchs, the career of Moses, the stirring episodes of the days of the judges, the rapid development of the times of Samuel, Saul, David, and Solomon, and of Elisha and Elijah are to be credited to men of the prophetic view-point. It is no less probable that the writers who wrought these groups of narratives into the stirring histories of Israel's growth which we know as the books of Judges, Samuel, and Kings were men of this type. History writing, then as now, was a ready and important method of preaching.

To minds familiar with such history, and trained, possibly, in producing it, the transition from such oral instruction as a religious adviser, as it is natural to credit to a Nathan, an Elijah, an Elisha, or an Amos, to the practice of recording the essential substance of such instruction or appeal, and of giving this circulation in written form, would not be very great. The messages would merely need to have a nationwide appeal and to be a challenge to the continuing thinking and habits of a whole people. A situation suited to the initiation of such a transition in method presented itself in the eighth century B. C. toward the close of the splendid reigns over Israel and Judah of the two notable sovereigns, Jeroboam II and Uzziah.

1. The Situation which Stirred the Soul of Amos.

It is generally agreed that the first of the new order of prophets to appear in public was Amos. From the historical and prophetic records of this period emerges a situation which accounts satisfactorily for the sudden appearance of a righteous individualist, such as Amos seems to have been, to interpret the apparent success and glory of his age in searching terms of morality and religion.

First of all, the lengthy and very prosperous reigns of Jeroboam and Uzziah had been days of peace, permitting the rapid acquisition of riches by those who were in positions of influence, and promoting the breaking down of the earlier democracy of society and simplicity of life which could no longer be maintained. Social injustice, careless rulers, arrogant leaders, legal unfairness, and the consequent crop of social evils seemed uncontrolled. There was much vulgar display and luxury, an unequal distribution of wealth, and vast social discontent.

Nominally, however, the people were as loyal as ever to Jehovah. Whenever business did not interfere, even the wealthy and proud were ready to keep up religious observances. Religion was not regarded by many, however, as something which should have the right of way in life. The leaders of society seemed money mad and pleasure bent. They had wealth and power, using each unscrupulously. The poor and weak had to endure with fortitude or patience what came their way.

Yet, behind this apparent breakdown of social and religious standards were the old religious fundamental conceptions, as old as Moses, to which a prophet could appeal. It was the reinforcement of these inbred convictions regarding Jehovah that gave the four prophets of the next half -century their wonderful power to reach the hearts of sinful, hard-hearted men and women.

But a second influence came to the help of these men of God who were seeking to stir the social conscience of the Hebrew peoples. A menace had appeared in the far North which brought a chill to patriotic hearts in Israel and Judah. It was still only a distant menace, yet a very real one. Assyria, the conquering nation which had levied tribute upon Omri and Ahab and had, in the latter half of the ninth century, broken the power of the Syrian kingdom whose capital was Damascus, was once more pushing its way steadily southward from the region of Carchemish with a vigor, fierceness, and success that was appalling. Damascus was still a buffer state, but men wondered how long before it would be absorbed by the insatiable conqueror and the southern boundary of Assyria become the northern boundary of Israel. The ruling classes in Israel and Judah put their trust in Jehovah, regarding their protection as His business, as long as they kept up generously His sacrifices and holy days (Amos 4:4, 5). The overwhelming of the two Hebrew peoples by the Assyrian foe seemed to mean an entire loss of their confidence in Jehovah, a religious collapse. It was the masterly reinterpretation of the whole situation in such a way as to show that it had come to be Jehovah's duty to bring this calamity to pass that saved Israel's faith in Him and initiated a new departure in religion.

2. What Made Amos a Prophet.

Amos declared that he was not a professional prophet (7: 14), but a farmer, an intelligent peasant landowner with a mind of his own. He was one of the sturdy, independent, self-respecting citizenry who were the secret of the vigor of the Hebrew race. He lived at Tekoa, not far from Bethel or Samaria, where he might have gone to sell his produce to the Phoenician traders. He had evidently pondered long and thoughtfully upon the social evils of his day and observed the wide difference between the religious professions of the people and the actual measure of their service to God, until he felt an irresistible impulse, which he ascribed to Jehovah, to give public expression to his convictions. Choosing, apparently, the date of some great feast which brought great throngs together at Bethel, Amos delivered publicly a series of brief but telling sermons to the Northern Israelites, which unquestionably searched the hearts of his listeners. Coming from an outsider, his stinging rebukes were bitterly resented by the leaders of the northern kingdom (7: 10-13). Amos was probably compelled to leave the scene and cross the border. Later, either he or some disciple reduced the substance of his sermons to written form for more general circulation. It is reasonable to think that they were widely read and that they influenced both Hosea and the youthful Isaiah.

3. His Messages to the People of the Northern Kingdom.

These can best be appreciated by a thoughtful reading of the book of Amos, guided by the outline below. The book, as we have it, contains the substance of a series of public addresses.

The superscription of the editor. Amos 1:1.

The prophet's text: Jehovah's voice is uplifted in judgment. 1: 2.

Jehovah must punish Israel's seven neighbor nations for their cruelty, greed, inhumanity, and disobedience. 1: 3-2:5.

Israel will be likewise held responsible for injustice, oppression, unchastity, greed, and the suppression of truth. None can escape the divine wrath. 2: 6-16.

Israel's relationship to Jehovah makes it the more necessary for Amos to denounce her. 3: 1-8.

Samaria's corruption would shock a Philistine or an Egyptian. Her punishment will be terribly severe. 3: 9-15.

Her great ladies, so frivolous and extravagant, will march away as captives. 4: 1-3.

Israel's religion is but transgression. She has ignored Jehovah's many hints to repent: hunger, drought, the locust, a pestilence. Be warned! The judgment will be sweeping. 4: 4-5: 3.

Israel might repent, but has gone too far in selfish wickedness. 5: 4-17.

The day of Jehovah will not be a day of deliverance but of bitter exile. 5: 18-27.

Those who persist in social selfishness are doomed. They will vainly seek Jehovah. 6: 1-14; 8: 4-14.

Five visions of Israel's impending fate: the locust plague, the devouring fire, the wall out of plumb, the over-ripe fruit, and the shattered altar. 7: 1-9; 8: 1-3; 9: 1-4.

Amaziah's attempt to expel Amos and the prophet's reply. 7: 10-17.

Jehovah's inescapable judgment. 9: 5-8a. [The scattering in exile will, however, be but a sifting out of the good grain. Eventually the Davidic dynasty will be supreme, and returned Israel will be prosperous and happy. 9: 8b-15.] **[1]**

4. The Distinctive Ideas of Amos.

One who reads with care these messages of Amos realizes clearly that the prophet is declaring (1) that Jehovah is a righteous Being, one who cannot overlook the social sins which wreck society and counteract religion; (2) that He expects His people to be righteous, showing it in deeds of goodness; (3) that Israel is hopelessly corrupt, shameless, defiant, and persistent; (4) that she has ignored divine warnings and is unlikely to repent; and (5) that Jehovah must bring upon her a sweeping judgment through the invasion of an army from the north (6: 14). The declaration of 9: 8b-15 that the predicted exile would result in a sifting out of the good grain, of the true Israel which would be restored and blessed, must be regarded as a later addition to the original book of Amos, which closed with 9: 8a. It is out of harmony with the sweeping declarations of the prophecy as a whole.

5. His Power and Its Limitations.

Amos affords an excellent example of a fact which every student of prophecy should keep in mind. His messages were very direct and powerful. They evidently made a deep impression upon the peoples of each kingdom. Yet he was a man of one idea. He applied the test of essential righteousness rigidly to daily life. Formal acts of worship offered by defiled hearts he declared to be unacceptable to God. That was a great assertion. It registered an important stage in religious thinking. Persistence in sin he regarded as demanding punishment. Beyond these simple principles Amos did not go. It would be rather unfair to expect to find a whole theology in the mind of an active farmer. However, Amos made one great, important idea stand out so clearly that it could neither be evaded nor forgotten. This was a great achievement.

[1] The use of brackets means that, in the judgment of the editors, the passage should be regarded as a later addition.

II - The Two Prophets of The Next Two Decades - Hosea of Israel and the Young Isaiah of Judah (740-722 B. C.)

In the eighth century before Christ, as now, no one personality was great enough to be God's sole channel of the truth needed by a people. Amos delivered a clear-cut, effective message, re-emphasizing a forgotten truth of great importance, yet the very fact that such criticism came from a man who belonged across the border in Judah may have been enough to cause many in the northern kingdom to ignore it. Fortunately, there was in that northern kingdom a kindred soul, named Hosea, who re-echoed the message of Amos in his own, more gracious fashion; and still another in Judah, a young prophet, Isaiah, who with yet wider ranging vision urged repentance and reform upon his beloved land of Judah and city of Jerusalem. These two, like Amos, realized the inexcusable social corruption of their peoples and regarded the oncoming Assyrian invader as the agent for Jehovah's use in arousing the dormant social and spiritual conscience of each people.

1. Hosea as Compared with Amos.

Hosea was evidently a man of considerable culture. He belonged to the city rather than the country. His means of support we may only conjecture; perhaps he was independent. He loved his country and its people, however sharply he accused them. He is the loving critic, an insider, a contrast in every way to Amos, the blunt, downright, strong-willed countryman from across the border. That such a man should be gripped by the same impulse to interpret the situation to his fellow citizens as he saw it was a matter of good fortune for them and for the world.

2. How Hosea Became a Prophet.

Hosea answers this question by declaring that Jehovah directed him to marry an unchaste woman by whom he had three children. Probably he did not know her real character at the outset, because he gave her his whole heart; but he recognized, later on, that the impulse to marry her had come from God. His wife, Gomer, deserted him, dragging his honor in the mire. She clearly deserved to be treated with rigor, yet he could not help continuing to love her. He found himself willing to forgive her, and, on repentance, to take her back. Somehow it flashed over Hosea's mind that what was true of him must be even more true of Jehovah, and that Gomer's unfaithfulness was paralleled by that of Israel to Israel's God. Hosea thus grasped a wonderful message. He became the prophet of God's inextinguishable love for His sinful people, just as Amos may be called the prophet of divine righteousness. His characterization of Jehovah as Israel's great-souled husband and tender guardian was only surpassed by the thought, as our Lord gave it expression, of God's fatherhood.

3. His Messages to His Own Countrymen.

Hosea's writings are far less intelligible than those of Amos. This was once explained by saying that Hosea wept as he wrote; a prosaic but more probable reason is that the Hebrew text is in bad condition.

The reader should read with all the greater care since Hosea well repays study. His prophetic declarations are a true gospel. Every great thinker echoed them, even Jesus.

The superscription of the editor. Hosea 1:1.

Hosea under divine direction marries an unchaste woman by whom he has three children, whose names convey God's attitude of severe displeasure with Israel. 1: 2-9.

[In due time Israel shall be restored to favor. 1: 10-2: 1.]

Israel, equally faithless to her husband, Jehovah, must be given a disciplinary experience. 2: 2-13.

But Jehovah will woo her back to faithfulness and loyalty. 2: 14-23.

Yet as Gomer had to be disciplined in seclusion, so Israel will have to be disciplined by exile. 3: 1-5.

The flagrant, incurable, blunderingly stubborn wickedness of Israel. 4: 1-19.

So great is Israel's ignorance and wilfulness that the impending judgment of Jehovah cannot be averted. 5: 1-14.

Realizing her plight, Israel may express repentance, but it will be superficial and useless; Jehovah demands real goodness and knowledge, but Israel's corruption is deep-seated and universal, most of all at court. 5: 15-7: 7.

She has no consistent policy; she is insincere and faithless; her men-made kings are impotent; her national life is decadent. 7:8-8: 14.

Exile, the destruction of her idolatrous shrines, and an invasion of armies shall be her lot. 9: 1-10: 15.

Jehovah has been a loving, tender Father and humane Master to Israel; she is ungrateful, yet He passionately longs to forgive her. 11: 1-11.

She has basely requited His love and care. 11: 12-12: 14.

Her idolatry and her forgetfulness of Jehovah is the just cause of her decay and ruin. 13: 1-16.

Israel, repent of your iniquity and pray Jehovah to show you His lovingkindness. 14: 1-3.

His answer will be prompt, generous, and effective. 14: 4-8.

An editorial "word to the wise." 14: 9.

4. The New and Permanent Element in Hosea's Messages.

Hosea, like Amos, was unsparing in his criticism of the national life. He believed that it was doomed. The state was to come to an end. But he set over against that act of justice the unchanging, inextinguishable love of Jehovah for His people, as shown in the past, and the character of His desires. These made it certain that the punishment would not be retributive in purpose, but redemptive and disciplinary. Eventually the nation would repent, be forgiven, and, once more, enter into loving, loyal relationship with Him. These three ideas the character of God as predominatingly loving, the redemptive purpose in His acts, and the obedient spirit sure to manifest itself eventually in Israel carry the religious thinker considerably beyond the range of Amos's

14

preaching. These ideas love, redemption, and obedience strike the truly spiritual notes in religion.

5. Isaiah's Call to Prophetic Work (Isaiah 6).

Quite possibly Hosea, when he felt an irresistible impulse to marry Gomer, was not aware that God had called him to be His prophet. It may have dawned upon him gradually that Jehovah had a purpose in leading him into his bitter domestic experience. It was otherwise with Isaiah. He knew the very hour and the spot when God laid hold upon him and charged him with the solemn and important but disheartening task of charging his fellow-Judeans with unrighteousness. It was during the last year of the reign of King Uzziah. In the temple Isaiah had a splendid vision of Jehovah enthroned in majesty, the Holy One, in whose presence he felt abased and unworthy (6). Comforted and made morally fit, Isaiah responded gladly to Jehovah's appeal for a messenger and undertook to convey His message to his fellow men. It was to be an unacceptable message of punitive judgment, he was told, one against which men would harden their hearts.

Isaiah was a complete contrast to his two predecessors. He was a man who loved Jerusalem, his home city. He unquestionably was as well-educated as a man of that age could be. He was an accomplished courtier and statesman, a man of large affairs. His range of ideas, the loftiness of his thought, his command of language and unrivalled power of terse, flaming description placed him in a literary class by himself. He could cast a spell over his listeners and sway them at will. As a leader Isaiah was without a rival. God raised him up to put religious thinking upon the broadest possible basis.

The book of Isaiah obviously falls into three general sections: (a) 1-35, (b) 36-39, and (c) 40-66. Of these (c) relates to the exile or later, (b) is paralleled by II Kings 18: 13-20: 20. Only (a) contains the portions which set forth the activity of the prophet. Even these chapters require much analysis and rearrangement to put them into a usable, chronological order, which gives us a picture of the work of the prophet.

6. Isaiah's Earliest Sermons to the People of Jerusalem (2: 5-4: i; 5: 1-24; 9: 8-10: 4; 5: 25-30; 17:1-11). About 738-739.

Isaiah, like his contemporaries, was impressed by the dangerously selfish corruption of the life of his day. His earliest utterances strike a strongly ethical note.

Jerusalem is superstitious, corrupt, frivolous, luxurious, inviting judgment. Isaiah 2: 5-4: 1.
Judah is the unfruitful vineyard of Jehovah. 5: 1-7.
Seven ' ' woes ' ' upon offenders against social righteousness . 5: 8-24.
Proud Ephraim shall be smitten, stroke after stroke, by war, disaster, anarchy, invasion, until she is swept away. 9:8-10:4; 5: 25-30.

Israel's bulwark, the Syrian kingdom, is doomed and Israel along with her. 17:1-11.

Here the prophet sounded a note like that of Amos. Jehovah in His righteousness would not condone such conditions. His condemnation was sure.

7. The Syro-Ephraimitish Crisis. About 735 B. C.

Foreign invasion, internal dissensions, and crushing tribute made a speedy end of the northern kingdom after the death of Jeroboam II. Hosea and Isaiah alike referred to the rapid dynastic changes, the social anarchy, the varied disaster, the futile appeals for foreign aid. In seven years there were four changes of dynasty and six rulers. Tiglath-pileser IV of Assyria was an aggressive foe, who seemed to contemplate the speedy conquest of Damascus. Pekah, of Israel, and Rezon, of Damascus, threatened to raid Judah in 735 B. C. in order to force Ahaz to join them in resisting the Assyrian king, or, failing in that compulsion, to depose him and set up a puppet king of their own choosing (Isaiah 7:6). The consequent panic of the king and people of Judah (7: 1, 2) brought Isaiah once more to the front.

8. Isaiah's Appeal to Ahaz (7: 1-25). About 735 B. C.

The prophet brought a message of encouragement to the king, who was inspecting his water-supply. The king's reception of his message led to another of a different sort.

These two nations are not to be feared; have faith in Jehovah's care, O Ahaz. Isaiah 7: 3-9.
Do you hypocritically reject [because of your own cherished purpose to appeal to Tiglath-pileser] Jehovah's sign? A young woman shall soon have a son, whom she will name Immanuel, showing her faith. The babe shall have enough, but those countries shall lie waste. 7: 10-16.
Unparalleled disaster will then come upon Judah. 7: 17-25.

Here a greater Isaiah is revealed. The name of his young son "Remnant shall return" shows that already the prophet saw far beyond the judgments he had predicted. His noble appeal to the king to trust in God and despise his foes and his confidence that the people would cherish such faith exhibit his strong religious leadership.

9. His Later Messages to the People (8:1-9:7). Before 732 B. C.

The appeal to Ahaz failed. The king preferred to pay heavily for Assyrian protection (II Kings 16: 7-9) and support. So the prophet had to state his case to the people. At this early period and throughout his career he based his policies upon the security of faith (30:15-18; 7:9, 13).

16

The two public predictions, on the sign-board and through the name given to the prophet's second son, of the fall of Damascus. Isaiah 8:1-4.

The rejection of Jehovah's gentle guidance means a brutal Assyrian domination. 8: 5-10.

He is a refuge to those who trust Him, but a terrible obstacle. 8:11-15.

Since my protests are unavailing, I with my children will bear testimony in silence. 8: 16-18.

However perplexed and distressed the days may become, there will be relief. The enemy's yoke will be broken by a righteous ruler with a fourfold name expressive of wisdom, prowess, success, and peace. 8: 19-9: 7.

These messages may cover several years. They announced the speedy downfall of Syria and Israel, which would mean eventually distress for Judah, from which in time she would find a glorious deliverance.

10. The Contributions of Isaiah to the Religious Thinking of This Early Period.

Isaiah's early sermons traversed the same situation as those of Amos and Hosea. He too faced a people in sore need of repentance and cleansing, idolatrous, luxurious, self-satisfied, selfish. Like those strong teachers, Isaiah had a vision of God, but his was greater than theirs. To him Jehovah was a Being whose characteristic quality was holiness. He meant it to include such qualities as righteousness, loving-kindness, and purity. In Isaiah's thinking holiness meant an absence of limitation, that Jehovah was a Being perfect in every respect. This holy Being desired His own people to be righteous, with abiding faith in Him. Their continuing failure to maintain true standards, Isaiah declared, was forcing Him to bring upon them a judgment of invasion. Like Hosea, Isaiah was not without hope. He named his eldest son "Remnant shall return" (7:3), in order to make him a walking prophecy of repentance. In his clear-headed mind the future appeared thus: (1) the richly deserved judgment, however severe and prolonged, would be disciplinary in ultimate purpose; (2) as an outcome there would be a "remnant." Judah, though cut down, would be a living stump (6:13); (3) this "remnant" would be faithful (7: 3 margin); (4) it would in time have its needed leadership, so as to be able to fulfil the Divine purposes (9: 2-7).

Thus Isaiah rounded out the thinking of his predecessors. Hosea saw a future. Isaiah made that future seem distinct and important.

II. The Interval of Relative Silence for Twenty-five Years.

Tiglath-pileser, of Assyria, with whom it was the policy of Ahaz to keep on friendly terms (implying, of course, some form of vassalage), died in 727 B. C. His successor, Shalmaneser IV, reigned just long enough to press to a successful close the war against the northern kingdom. His great successor, Sargon (722-705), received the actual submission of Samaria and executed Shalmaneser's plans (II Kings 17: 6). Sargon was a capable soldier and sovereign. Ahaz remained loyal to Assyria throughout these changes. He may have deeply resented Isaiah's disapproval of his policy and shown his royal displeasure by depriving the prophet of his freedom of speech. At all events Isaiah was in obscurity during the whole long reign. The death of Ahaz in 715 B. C. placed Hezekiah on the throne of Judah. Young, earnest, and promising, the new king was friendly to Isaiah, although he may not have agreed entirely with the prophet on matters political. His accession placed Isaiah in the important position of privy-counsellor to the king. He became a trusted and influential factor in the life of the nation.

III - The Two Prophets of the Reign of Hezekiah - Micah the Commoner and Isaiah The Statesman (715-686 B. C.)

When Hezekiah ascended the throne of Judah, restoring Isaiah to royal favor and giving him freedom to function as a friend and adviser of the people, another leader appeared in Judah who was much of a kindred spirit, the prophet Micah. How Micah came into the circle of influence is nowhere stated. He seems to have been another keenly observant countryman, like Amos, with a stinging message of judgment upon the leaders of the people of Judah, whose social crimes he pitilessly exposed. Like Hosea and Isaiah, however, he had also a gracious message regarding Jehovah's ways with men and concerning His plans.

1. Micah's Vision of Doom in View of the Social Sins of Judah's Leaders (Micah 1-3; 6: 9-7: 6).

To give an exact date to these chapters is impracticable. They are probably to be dated in the early reign of Hezekiah (Jeremiah 26: 18, 19), but may be as late as 703-701 B. C.

The superscription of the editor. Micah 1:1.
The doom of Samaria will extend to Jerusalem. 1: 2-9.
With what accompanying distresses the conquering army is advancing from the seacoast (told in paronomasias)! 1: 10-16.
The greedy, unscrupulous, self-deceived Judeans of wealth and power will suffer deserved exile. 2: 1-1!
[The remnant will be delivered from the exile. 2: 12-13.] Judah is as wicked as Israel was. 6: 9-7: 6.
Judah's rulers are so heartless and her false prophets so blinded, and all so united in their corruption that a sweeping judgment is sure. 3: 1-12.

It is interesting to note that Micah's rebukes awakened the popular con science and led to public repentance, so that the judgment, in the mind of men of the next century, became unnecessary (Jeremiah 26:17-19).

2. The Growing Political Unrest of Judah: Isaiah's Warning (Isaiah 20).

When Samaria fell in 722 B. C. Sargon had just ascended the throne of Assyria. He was a capable ruler, his empire under full control. But for a decade he was busied with affairs in other parts of his dominion and paid little attention to Palestine. The Philistine king of Ashdod, with other kinglets, trusting in the promises of aid from Egypt, revolted against Sargon. This insurrection, so close at hand, stirred the people of Judah. Isaiah was strongly opposed to their joining in it, and expressed his advice by a striking object lesson. For the three years from 713 to 711 he walked the streets of Jerusalem in the garb of a captive, as much as to say "Assyria will take away captive both Egypt and all who trust in her." Needless to say, the Judean revolt did not take place.

3. Isaiah's Opposition to an Alliance Against Sennacherib (Isaiah 18:1-19:17; 28-32). About 703 B. C.

Sargon died in 705 B. C. The accession of Sennacherib to the throne of Assyria was the signal over the whole empire for the wide-spread explosion of the long-subdued but passionate desire for freedom from Assyrian dominance. Among others, the little peoples of Palestine, encouraged by Shabako, the Ethiopian king of Egypt, and by Merodach-baladan of Chaldea (II Kings 20:12-19), formed a coalition into which Judah was gradually drawn in spite of Isaiah's earnest opposition. His vigorous appeals at this time are embodied in chapters 28-32, which set forth the contrast between Jehovah's real purpose and the foolish schemes of the politicians of Judah.

Let the Ethiopian ambassadors go back; Jehovah is biding His time. Isaiah 18. Like the drunken leaders of beautiful Samaria are those of Judah. They resent my reiterated warnings, and place their security in rites. The only safe and broad basis for our national hope is righteousness and justice. 28: 1-22.

God adjusts His processes to the ends He has in view. 28: 23-29.

Jerusalem is God's altar-hearth; she shall be inviolable. 29: 1-8.

The people are unreceptive to my appeals; they even try to hide their plots from Jehovah's eyes. 29: 9-24.

The alliance with Egypt will only bring disgrace: she is "Rahab sit-still." 30:1-7.

You rebelliously minded people wish only agreeable words to be spoken to you; utter ruin will befall you. 30: 8-17.

At the crisis of distress Jehovah will have mercy and bring again prosperity. 30: 18-26.

Jehovah will appear in His wrath to annihilate Assyria, while Judah rejoices. 30: 27-33.

Woe to those who trust in Egypt: Jehovah will protect His people and destroy Assyria. 31: 1-9.

Egypt will receive the judgment she merits. 19: 1-17.

There shall sometime be a king governing righteously. 32: 1-8.

The frivolous wealthy women of Jerusalem will soon have abundant sorrow. 32: 9-14.

Righteous conduct and justice will bring peace and happiness. 32: 15-20.

The crisis developed Isaiah's ripest thinking regarding Jehovah's greatness, the wisdom of trusting in Him, the folly of reliance upon Egypt or any other human aid, the importance of true personality, the quiet assurance of the man of faith, and the absolute certainty of the execution of the Divine purposes and plans. When he faced a distressing present, it never caused him to lose sight of the certain future.

4. Isaiah's Assurances of Jerusalem's Deliverance from Sennacherib's Unjustifiable Attack (701-690 B. C.).

In spite of Isaiah's efforts the people of Judah did join the coalition in revolting against Sennacherib. Hezekiah was made the general leader. Sennacherib, in due time, about 701 B. C., was ready to attend to his rebellious subjects in "the westland." With a large army he marched across the Euphrates, then southward, crushing all opposition as he advanced. An Egyptian army did march out to meet him, but was crushed at Eltekeh in southern Philistia. He then ravaged Judah and besieged Jerusalem.

Judah's distress is due to her own faithlessness and ingratitude Jehovah demands justice and mercy and obedience. The city is degenerate. Isaiah 1: 2-26.

The unpardonable frivolity of the people threatened by such danger. 22: 1-14.

The ambitious steward, Shebna, deposed in favor of the steadfast Eliakim. 22:15-25.

Hezekiah came to terms. He purchased the freedom of the city by paying a very heavy ransom (II Kings 18:13-16).

Later on Sennacherib apparently determined that he must gain control of Jerusalem, which was a very strong city. He sent his officers, in violation of his plighted word, to demand its surrender. Isaiah now supported Hezekiah in his refusal to comply with the demand (II Kings 18:17-19:7). He believed that Jehovah would not permit Jerusalem to be destroyed.

The power of Assyria shall soon be broken: Jehovah's great deed of deliverance will give His people peace; Jerusalem shall be preserved inviolate. Isaiah 33.

The proud and boastful Assyrian is only Jehovah's tool: his humiliating ruin is sure. 10: 5-34.

The Assyrian will be defeated: Jehovah's rule is worldwide. 14: 24-27.

Thus the prophet steadied the faith of king and people in this fateful crisis. It was a wonderful example of the power of personality. Hezekiah was firm. Either at once or later Sennacherib seems to have made a second demand with a similar lack of success. Just then he was forced to march toward Egypt.

There his army was smitten by a pestilence, which he, of course, interpreted as due to the dangerous anger of the gods of the invaded countries. In exact accordance with the prediction of II Kings 19: 32-34 he returned to Assyria, where, considerably later, he was murdered.

5. Sermons from the Later Life of Isaiah and Micah.

To the years succeeding this great triumph of the sovereign and his honored prophet must be attributed Hezekiah's reformation. The influence of Isaiah must have been very great. To these happy years may be attributed, without any real certainty, some beautiful passages in the writings attributed to Isaiah and to Micah. They serve to round out the thinking of the age, and seem appropriate to a period when these two great religious thinkers had the leisure and the motive for dwelling upon the implications of their earlier predictions.

Isaiah's story of his call to his prophetic task. Isaiah 6. Jerusalem shall be the teaching center of true religion for the world. Isaiah 2: 2-4; Micah 4: 1-5.

Little Bethlehem in the country shall be the birthplace of the expected leader. Micah 5: 2-5a.

The religion which Jehovah demands is reasonable. Micah 6: 1-8.

The shoot from the stock of Jesse shall rule in righteousness and peace. Isaiah 11: 1-9.

The Jerusalem of that ideal day. Isaiah 4: 2-6.

The task of the deliverer and of the "remnant." Micah 5: 5b-15.

[Repentant Israel's confession of faith. Micah 7: 7-20.]

[The second great deliverance and return. Isaiah 11: 10-16.]

6. The Leading Ideas of the Four Eighth-Century Prophets.

The half -century during which the four prophets delivered their messages was not a time of continuous activity. Rather, there were bursts of prophetic activity during the earlier and the later years, each in connection with a great national peril. Fortunately, there were four interpreters of the divine personality and purpose, instead of one. Amos, Hosea, Isaiah, and Micah had as many different view-points, yet their messages fit into a fairly clear group of declarations which had the important effect of altering the emphasis in religion from ritualistic regularity to the maintenance of moral and spiritual character and the rendering of genuine service to society.

The outstanding ideas of this first important era of prophecy may be stated as follows:

(1) Jehovah is to be described in terms of character rather than power. He is righteous, loving, holy.

(2) He insists that His people shall also lay stress on character. His demands are wholly reasonable.

(3) His people, especially the responsible leaders, exhibit all sorts of social, economic, and religious wickedness.

21

(4) Notwithstanding frequent divine warnings they are obstinately impenitent.

(5) Hence Jehovah, in order to awaken the public conscience, must bring upon the land the calamity of Assyrian invasion.

(6) His purpose in this will be redemptive and disciplinary; hence there will be a "remnant."

(7) Through the leadership which Jehovah will eventually provide the remnant will execute His great purpose for the world.

(8) Jerusalem will become the religious center of the world.

7. The Limitations of This Prophecy.

Much of this teaching is as sound to-day as it was twenty-eight centuries ago. Our social conditions compare closely with the conditions described by these prophets. City and community problems are more or less eternal. Selfishness, pride, greed, and the love of power work havoc with true religion in all ages. The ideas of God still hold good. But the prophets of the eighth century B. C. were limited in two marked ways. They could not imagine Jehovah as carrying out His plans for the world except by using the Hebrew nation as His working unit. Hence they looked forward to its literal and complete restoration as a nation, with Jerusalem functioning as the capital and the temple as the religious center. Moreover, they expected that the world would receive its knowledge of Jehovah by coming to Jerusalem, His abode. These ideas were glorious and commendable, but not truly interpretative of the real Divine intention. They were a sort of bridge between the older, narrow nationalism and the true universalism of a century or two later.

These prophets were really predicting that the whole world would ultimately worship Jehovah. They erred only in specifying the exact method by which this was to be brought about. It took nearly two centuries of added experience to reveal the real Divine method.

IV - The Two Prophets of the Reform Movement of Josiah's Reign - Zephaniah and the Young Jeremiah (626-621 B. C.)

The death of Hezekiah placed his young son, Manasseh, upon the throne of Judah. The new sovereign quickly fell under the baleful influence of those who hated the prophetic circle and were eager to break its hold upon the people. Isaiah and Micah disappeared from notice; possibly they were slain. The prophets and their sympathizers were sorely persecuted; blood ran freely. Prevented thus from public teaching or preaching, the prophets turned their energies gradually in the direction of literature preserving, editing, producing. They quickly discovered that a writing could preach very successfully, passing from hand to hand.

During the long reign of Manasseh (686-641 B. C.) Assyrian influence was paramount in Judah. This was not disadvantageous in many respects. It promoted a return of prosperity and a real development culturally. It also involved, however, the popularization of Assyrian religious customs and the revival of Canaanitish practices. The outcome of the half-century was a better-organized prophetic group and a people religiously decadent but quite prosperous. Under these conditions Manasseh's grandson, Josiah, ascended the throne about 639 B. C.

1. The Young King and His Advisers.

Josiah was only eight years of age when he became the king of Judah. As he grew from childhood to maturity he came under the helpful influence of those with high ideals, such men as Zephaniah the prophet, Shaphan the royal scribe and Hilkiah the high priest. He did not take revenge upon those who had opposed the prophets, but was encouraged by his advisers to undertake definite and needed improvements, first of all a repairing of the Temple. This act of itself meant an honoring of Jehovah and an encouragement of His loyal worship.

2. The New, Menacing, Northern Foe.

Assyria had by this time been an acknowledged suzerainty so long that her relationship to Judah was unquestioned by the Hebrews. Asurbanipal of Assyria died, however, in 626 B. C., after a brilliant reign of forty-two years. For some years previous his grip had slackened. From the reform sermons of Zephaniah and Jeremiah we have hints of the fears inspired in some of the Palestinian peoples by the prospect of the descent of fierce and warlike marauders from the north (Jeremiah 6: 22-26; 4: 29). Herodotus is the authority for the statement that the Scythians at this time poured down, like predatory Cossack hordes, through Asia Minor over many parts of the Assyrian empire, doing vast damage everywhere. As in the preceding century, the prophets viewed these invaders as destined by Jehovah to punish His faithless people, unless they repented promptly.

3. How Zephaniah Became a Prophet.

At this time of crisis in the empire the prophet Zephaniah sounded a stirring note of reform in Jerusalem and Judah. Of him nothing is known except that he was the great-great-grandson of Hezekiah (1: 1). If this means that he was of royal lineage, it accounts for his early influence at the court of Josiah. Like Amos and Isaiah, he felt called upon to denounce the social and religious condition of his country and the foreign influences and customs which had undermined the national religious life and the standards of the people.

4. His Announcement of Doom for Unrepentant Judah (About 626 B. C.).

The superscription of the editor. Zephaniah 1:1.

Jehovah's sweeping judgment about to dispose of] Judah's idolaters and apostates. 1: 2-6.

The "day of Jehovah" will be a day of wrath, terrible in its distresses, unsparing of any. 1: 7-18.

Only the meek and righteous may escape. 2: 1-3.

The judgment will fall upon Philistia, Ethiopia and Assyria, whose proud confidence will be shaken. 2: 4-7, 12-15.

[Moab and Ammon for their arrogance shall be destroyed. 2: 8-11.]

Jerusalem's proud, impenitent rulers and teachers shall be expelled, but the righteous "remnant," honest and peaceful, shall remain. 3: 1-13.

Jehovah will then dwell among his people, rejoicing over them. 3: 14-17.

[After the exile all shame and reproach shall be turned into universal praise and glory. 3: 18-20.]

5. Zephaniah 's Austere Gospel.

Zephaniah must have been young, hence the unsparing sweep of his vision of Jehovah's wrath. He is a prophet of doom, "searching out sinners for destruction." This judgment is a world judgment. He insists, however, with his great predecessors, that moral qualities have a permanent value, hence a "remnant" will remain. Many scholars regard Zephaniah as probably incapable of assuming the mood of rejoicing expressed in 3: 14-17. Such think that these verses are, like 2: 8-11 and 3: 18-20, a post-exilic addition to Zephaniah's own prophecies.

6. The Call of Jeremiah to Prophetic Duty (Jeremiah i). About 625 B. C.

How Jeremiah was convinced that Jehovah had laid His commands upon him is not clear. He was of a priestly family (1:1), and very much alive to the danger which threatened the land through the feared Scythians (1: 13, 14). His growing sense of duty overmastered his feeling of immaturity and his natural shyness, God giving him a growing sense of His resourcefulness and might.

Superscription of the editor. Jeremiah 1: 1-3.

Jeremiah's call to prophetic service. 1: 4-10.

His reassuring vision of the blossoming almond. "Jehovah is watchful." 1: 11, 12. The vision of the boiling kettle, symbolizing the fiery flood of judgment. "Be bold; you shall be secure." 1: 13-19.

7. His Early Sermons Urging Repentance and Reform in Judah (625-621 B. C.).

Jeremiah's first appeals to the people recall Hosea's pleas. He used the figure of marriage to represent the bond between Jehovah and His people, and reviewed with startling frankness their repeated infidelities.

Notwithstanding the faithlessness of Israel, Jehovah's bride, to Him, Jehovah will gladly forgive her, if repentant. Jeremiah 2:1-4:4.

Through the terrible northern foe (4: 6-8; 5: 15-19; 6: 22, 23), so devastating, Jehovah will bring judgment upon sinful Jerusalem, which rejects His teaching. 4: 5-6: 30.

Such powerful appeals as these and those of Zephaniah must have predisposed the people to thoughtfulness. When the "book of the law" was found (II Kings 22) and read publicly, and when King Josiah led his subjects in accepting its demands, they responded as a nation, adopting very sweeping reforms (621 B. C.).

8. Twelve Years of Life Under the New Law.

The Deuteronomic law in itself must have been approved by Jeremiah. Its spirit of philanthropic friendliness was like his own. Jeremiah 11: 1-8 seems to record his active support of the new covenant. With its emphasis of the ritualistic side of religion, however, he was not likely to be in fullest sympathy. It may be significant that unless, Jeremiah 31: 2-30, a prediction of the restoration of northern Israel is assigned to this period, Jeremiah seems to have been silent.

From the standpoint of the state these years were noteworthy. The people followed their king. He enlarged his territory, was quite free to follow his own plans because of Assyria's growing weakness, and prospered.

9. The Death of Josiah at Megiddo (608 B. C.).

Meanwhile in Egypt a strong king had arisen who began to have visions of wresting from weakening Assyria the leadership of western Asia. At least Necho intended to control Palestine and Syria. He enlisted a large contingent of Greek mercenaries, making his own army formidable. On his northward march at Megiddo Josiah disputed his advance but was readily overthrown and slain. The prophetic party which had been in control in Judah placed Shallum, a promising son of Josiah, on the throne of Judah, naming him Jehoahaz. After three months Jehoahaz was summoned by Necho to Riblah in northern Syria, deposed, and sent as a captive to Egypt, where he died. The bitter disappointment of Jeremiah was expressed in Jeremiah 22: 10-12. In place of Jehoahaz Necho appointed Jehoiakim, a brother, but of an opposite type.

V - The Three Prophets of Jehoiakim's Reign- Nahum, Jeremiah and Habakkuk (608-597 B. C.)

The accession of Jehoiakim made a rapid change in Judean conditions. The new king was self-centered and unprincipled. He favored the ways of Manasseh, his grandfather, rather than those of Josiah, his father. The prophetic party lost its influence; Jeremiah, its leader, suffered much ill-treatment and even danger. These difficulties, which the prophet felt acutely, only made him persist in his prophetic duty at all costs. The eleven years of Jehoiakim's reign was a period of martyrdom for Jeremiah, but it taught him the realities of religion. He had to fall back upon Jehovah as his one sure support.

1. The Paean of Nahum Over the Anticipated Downfall of Nineveh.

The actual date of Nahum's brief announcement of Nineveh's fate is uncertain. It must have appeared during the period when the great empire was weakening rapidly. Any date after Asurbanipal's death in 626 B. C. would be possible, but the clear assurance of the poem that at last Assyria's ruin is at hand points to a date about 608 B. C., just before the actual capture of the city in 606 B. C.

Superscription of the editor. Nahum 1:1.
Jehovah's goodness and His sternness assure His judgment of the wicked and His care for Judah. 1: 2-15; 2: 2.
The capture and plunder of Nineveh, the lair of the old lion, is at hand. 2:1,3-13. Bloody, deceitful Nineveh, like Thebes before her, will go to ruin.
Who will lament her? 3: 1-19.

This vivid poem was no mere cry for vengeance. It expressed the just measure of ruin which Assyria's long career of savagery and greed had brought upon her. Once weakened she could but expect destruction. To a Judean the passing of Assyria seemed the opening of a new future.

2. Jeremiah's Bitter Experiences but Brave Persistence During the Early Reign of Jehoiakim (608-605 B. C.).

The ostracism and active hatred which Jeremiah felt so keenly arose, probably, out of the attitude of the king, but it found expression nearer home. His own neighbors sought his life. Such bitter experiences deeply puzzled and pained the prophet. [1]

The conspirators against Jeremiah to be dealt with by Jehovah. Jeremiah 11: 9-23.

26

"O Jehovah, why give such men prosperity?" [Answer.] "You have worse trials to face than their opposition." 12: 1-6.

At the house of the potter: Jehovah is as free in dealing with a nation as the potter in shaping clay. 18. A temple sermon: This temple will be destroyed, like that at Shiloh, if Judah's social sins persist. 7: 1-8: 3; 26.

Persistently corrupt Judah's inevitable fate. 8: 4-10: 25.

Symbolic declarations of judgment: the waist-cloth and the wine jars. 13: 1-14.

"O Jehovah, why compel me to suffer so unjustly?" 20:7-18. Jeremiah assured of God's continuing and precious fellowship. 15: 10-21.

How he learned through his afflictions to place his trust in Jehovah alone. 16: 1-17: 18.

The broken water-jar a warning of the destructive judgment of Jehovah. 19: 1-20: 6.

The writing, destruction, and remaking of the collection of Jeremiah's early sermons. 36; 45.

This grievous testing which Jeremiah endured somehow revealed to him, as indicated in 15: 10-17: 18, the supreme privilege and joy of knowing God and being close to Him. It was such another creative experience as that of Hosea.

3. Jeremiah's Joy Over Egypt's Overthrow by Nebuchadrezzar, the Chaldean Prince (605 B. C.).

Nineveh fell in 606 B. C. at the hands of the Medes and the Chaldeans. The Chaldeans took Syria and Palestine as a part of their share of the Assyrian empire. Nabopolassar of Chaldea lost no time iri sending an army under the crown prince, Nebuchadrezzar, to meet Pharaoh-Necho. The armies met at Carchemish. The Egyptians were decisively defeated, and Judah thereby passed automatically under the political control of Chaldea (II Kings 24: 7).

A taunt song: the boastful Pharaoh with his contingents has received a wounding not easily assuaged. Jeremiah 46: 2-12.

"My long continued ministry has failed to bring about repentance: the Chaldeans will be the executors of divine judgment for seventy years." 25: 1-14.

The wine cup of Jehovah's wrath shall be drunk by other peoples. 25: 15-38; (46: 13-49:39 reproduces later, fuller declarations).

4. The Meditations of Habakkuk on God's Moral Ordering of the Situation (Habakkuk 1-3).

The actual date of the prophecy of Habakkuk is rather uncertain. It belongs to the period of the Chaldean overlordship, but is dated by many students about 560 B. C., during the exile, instead of 608 B. C. At any rate the prophet was like-minded with Jeremiah in his attitude toward Divine methods in dealing with the world. He vindicated God's character by stressing the essential permanence of righteousness.

The swift and terrible Chaldeans are the agents of Jehovah's just judgments against wrongdoing. Habakkuk 1: 1-11.
Shall Jehovah, the Holy One, make use of so inhuman, so insatiable a nation? 1:12-17.
The Divine answer: wickedness is weakness; true righteousness is morally and spiritually permanent. 2: 1-4.
A five-fold woe upon the persistent evil-doer. 2: 5-20. [A lyric describing Jehovah's march from Sinai to redeem his people. 3.]

This unknown prophet expressed a great, illuminating idea, which undergirds all human moral advance. An organization for plunder is sure to weaken eventually, whereas the righteous man can afford to wait and work, knowing that what he stands for must prevail. Jeremiah 12: 1-^4 and Habakkuk raise a question which later writers in the Old Testament discuss frequently.

5. Jeremiah's Preaching During the Last Few Years of Jehoiakim's Reign (601-597 B. C.).

For several years Jehoiakim paid tribute regularly to the Chaldeans (II Kings 24: 1). Why he rebelled against them is uncertain, probably on account of Egyptian promises of help. Nebuchadrezzar was not ready at once to lead an army into Palestine, but he was alert. He ordered the troops and auxiliaries (II Kings 24: 2) which were in the region of revolt to do all possible damage to Judah. Their raids caused the Rechabites to take refuge in Jerusalem. At this crisis Jeremiah, who had been quiet for several peaceful years, again appeared to appeal to the people.

Jeremiah's estimate of royal duty and of Jehoiakim's execution of it. Jeremiah 21: 11-22: 9, 13-19.
Judah's unfortunate pride and disobedience promises inevitable ruin. 13: 15-27.
The drought in Judah and Jeremiah's intercession. 14: 1-15: 9.
Jehovah mourns over the devastation of his land and will requite it. 12: 7-17.
How the Rechabites served Jeremiah as an object lesson of real loyalty. 35.

Jeremiah attributed the troubles which overwhelmed his people to their rulers and to their own shortcomings. They had almost driven Jehovah away from His own land. Such splendid loyalty as that of the Rechabites would insure God's continuing blessing.

6. The Religious Values of Jehoiakim's Eleven Years.

Jehoiakim's hostility to Jeremiah did one great service to religion. The prophet's lot was a very hard one, so much so that he cried out against it. His loneliness threw him back onto God and gave him a growing sense of personal fellowship with the Divine which was a virtual discovery in religion. He saw the fallacies of the public policies; he stood up against false leadership; he saw the hand of Jehovah in current history and was persistent in pointing out the doom toward which the nation was drifting. He was gentle, yet finely loyal and noble, standing before the very throne of God with appeals for reasonable treatment. Discovering himself as a personality in close touch with God, he was ready to make the yet greater discovery of the place of the individual in God's plans. These years, hard as they were, meant much to the world.

7. The First Exile (597 B. C.).

In 597 Nebuchadrezzar's army from Babylon invested Jerusalem. At this juncture Jehoiakim died. He was succeeded by Coniah, his eighteen-year-old son, who took the royal name of Jehoiachin. The young ruler promptly surrendered. The conqueror deported to Babylon the royal family, the court, the important leaders of the state, and many of the working classes. Probably his purpose was to take away those likely to lead a revolt. Another son of Josiah, Zedekiah, was left upon the throne.

[1] From this point on the reader will note that the references to Jeremiah's preaching follow a puzzling order. The order chosen is that in which the sermons were preached. How they came to be rearranged as they are is one of the mysteries of the Old Testament.

VI - The Messages of Jeremiah And Ezekiel Regarding the Fall of Jerusalem During the Reign of Zedekiah Over Judah (597-586 B. C.)

With the enthronement of Zedekiah began a period for Jeremiah which was less strenuous yet deeply disappointing. The king had good impulses, but a weak will. He was surrounded by inexperienced, headstrong advisers against whom Jeremiah could accomplish little. The prophet had the sorrow of realizing that his beloved country and its institutions were being wrecked. His own faith in Jehovah and willingness to follow His leading no one else seemed to share.

1. Jeremiah's Vigorous Appeals During the First Five Years (597-592 B. C.).

His letter to the restless captives in Babylonia: Settle down; heed not false advisers; your captivity will be long. Jeremiah 29.

His vivid comparison of the exiled Judeans with their worthless brethren left in Judah. 24.

His denunciation of the false prophetic leaders, so superficially optimistic, so lacking in real conviction, supporters of evil. 23: 9-40.

His public, symbolical appeal to the ambassadors and to Judah against an alliance against Babylon. 27.

His strenuous encounter with Hananiah, the leader of the opposition. 28.

A warning to keep the Sabbath. [1] 17: 19-27.

2. The Call of Ezekiel, the Priest, to Prophetic Service in Babylonia (592 B. C.).

Among those who were carried away captive to Babylonia in 597 by Nebuchadrezzar was Ezekiel, a young man of priestly descent and training. He was approximately thirty years of age, broadly cultured, versatile, a thoughtful and able leader. God called him to the work of a prophet through a remarkable experience, which he recounted later in interesting detail.

Ezekiel's vision of the omnipotent, omnipresent, omniscient Jehovah on His throne, guarded by the four living creatures. Ezekiel 1: 1-28.

His Divine commission to deliver a message of doom to his disbelieving and stubborn people. 2: 1-3: 15.

His appointment also as a personal watchman and pastor. 3: 16-27.

The vision which Ezekiel saw was really indescribable. There is a reverence and reticence about his sketch which overbears the grotesque and gives the whole conception dignity. It was the Divine majesty in all its splendor which laid him prostrate, then charged him with a great responsibility.

3. His Early Ministry to the Judean Exiles in Babylonia (592-586 B. C.).

Ezekiel's principal task during the next five or six years was that of convincing the exiles that Jerusalem and the Temple were doomed. They could not bring themselves to believe this. Jehovah's own prestige in the world seemed to guarantee the contrary. Jerusalem was His own city; the Temple was His abode; the monarchy He had created; they seemed inviolable, all the more because Isaiah had so declared over a century earlier (see page 26). Moreover, there were other prophets, those whose declarations Jeremiah had often contradicted, who were constantly making hopeful assertions, far more palatable to their countrymen. Hence, during these few years before the actual destruction of Jerusalem, Ezekiel's lot, like that of Jeremiah before him, was unenviable.

Four symbolical predictions (drawing a picture of a siege, lying on his side a day for each year of exile, baking and eating famine bread, shaving his body clean) of the certain fate of Jerusalem. Ezekiel 4:1-5: 17.

Religious abominations doomed. 6: 1-7: 27. Jerusalem's abominable idolatries warranting a pitiless slaughter, a burned city, the rebuking of its guilty rulers and the departure of Jehovah. 8:1-11:25. The folly of the popular deference paid to the shallow, time-serving prophets and the disregard of genuine prophetic leaders. 12: 1-14:11. Jerusalem, like a useless vine, burned at both ends, is only fit for destruction. 15.

The shameful moral record of Jerusalem, Jehovah's bride. 16.

Her faithless king, Zedekiah, and the certain destruction of his kingdom. 17.

The principles of Divine procedure: retribution is for sin; each individual determines his own destiny and must bear the consequences. 18.

A few righteous inhabitants will not save a guilty land. 14: 12-23.

The rulers of Judah have not saved the state. 19.

Israel's persistent idolatry will not prevent Jehovah from carrying through His purposes. 20: 1-44.

The sharpened sword of Jehovah's agent. 20: 45-21: 32.

The classes and the masses in Jerusalem equally sinful. 22.

The entangling alliances of Samaria and Jerusalem a warning to the world. 23.

Jerusalem a rusty kettle to be cleansed only by fire. 24: 1-14.

The sudden death of Ezekiel's wife a tragic earnest of the stunning calamity soon to be realized by the captives. 24: 15-27.

Ezekiel rendered a remarkable service to his people during these years. He used his varied abilities with wonderful skill to bring about a change of popular conviction regarding Jehovah's attitude to his people, which would enable them to endure the shock of the downfall of what they held most dear. His insistence on the goodness and grace of God (18: 23, 31, 32) and his clear development of the idea that the individual is the responsible unit with which God deals (18: 4-18) were real contributions to religious advance.

4. Jeremiah's Declarations in Connection with the Fall of Jerusalem (588-586 B. C.).

In 588 B. C. a new, ambitious king, Hophra, ascended the throne of Egypt. He joined with the little peoples of Palestine in urging Zedekiah and his advisers to renounce allegiance to Chaldea. In spite of what Jeremiah could do the revolt took place. Both Jeremiah and Ezekiel denounced this act as treachery to Jehovah Himself (Ezekiel 17: 19). By the end of the year the Chaldean army appeared in Palestine and began the reconquest of the whole area. For over a year Jerusalem, a secure fortress, held out bravely. Its defenders kept hoping for Egyptian aid, but the army sent by Hophra was quickly defeated. From the first Jeremiah declared that unconditional surrender was the only hope of the people.

Jeremiah's reply to Zedekiah's query whether Jehovah would deliver the city: There is no hope; surrender only will save life. Jeremiah 21: 1-10.

His later advice: The city will be taken. (Surrender and) you shall be given royal clemency and favor. 34: 1-7.

His denunciation of the breach of faith toward the liberated slaves on the part of the princes and people. 34: 8-22.

His bold, symbolical prediction of the certain return of the exiles to Judah. 32 (especially verses 6-15).

Since Jeremiah was steadily declaring the loss of all immediate hope for the city or people, it was a striking prediction of a future restoration, when he not only purchased a plot of land, but took pains to comply publicly with every detail of legal procedure regarding its registration.

5. Jeremiah's Prophecies of a Spiritualized Future.

Jeremiah had come to the point of contemplating an entire ending of city, Temple and kingdom. Like a true prophet, however, he believed as firmly as ever in Jehovah's power and in His purpose. He was consequently led to take a great forward step in religious thinking. He declared that God in the future would use the individual as His working unit, not the nation. It could go to pieces, yet God's purpose would be carried on by godly disciples acting collectively, a congregation rather than a body-politic.

A new record of prophetic interpretation to be prepared. Jeremiah 30: 1-4.
Jehovah's "day" to be eventually a day of deliverance. 30: 5-17.
Ephraim to be restored also to prove Jehovah's goodness and loving-kindness. 30: 18-31: 20.
Ephraim and Judah alike will then rejoice. 31: 21-26.
In those days each individual shall be responsible for himself. 81: 27-30.
Jehovah's new covenant will be written on each heart. 31: 31-34 (compare 3: 14-18).
Jehovah Himself will be the assurance of new Israel's permanence. 31: 35-40.
Peace will come by and by to Jerusalem, now besieged and desolated. 33: 1-13.
Jehovah will raise up a righteous BRANCH to rule over the righteous nation under a promise which is unbreakable. 33:14-26.

These chapters make the transition from religion limited to a particular area or people to a genuinely spiritual religion with no such limits. A religiously minded individual or a group of such people are movable. They can be truly religious anywhere. With the clear declaration of individualism by Jeremiah and Ezekiel to be credited to the former because his experiences opened the way for its realization a real missionary interpretation of religion was finally made possible. It was another religious discovery of the first importance.

6. Ezekiel's Oracles Against the Nations Which Seemed to Block Judah's Way.

These declarations about Judah's near neighbors and the greater Asiatic powers were not put forth necessarily at any one time, but may be most appropriately considered at this juncture. They probably date before 585 B. C.

Against Ammon, Moab, Edom and Philistia for petty spitefulness. Ezekiel 25.

32

Against Tyre, whose capture by Nebuchadrezzar will be mourned by her rivals. 26.

Tyre, the gallant, costly, beautiful trireme of the seas, laden with the riches of the world, shall be a total wreck. 27.

Tyre had every opportunity: with Sidon she must suffer. 28: 1-24.

Egypt, the fallen cedar, the turbulent crocodile, will meet the fate of other great world empires. 29-32.

At last restored Israel will acknowledge Jehovah. 28: 25, 26.

7. Jeremiah's Policy at the Fall of the City (586 B.C.).

In July, 586, a breach was at last made in the wall of the city. King Zedekiah tried to escape but was captured. The city and Temple were plundered and burned; the walls were broken down; many more citizens were carried away captive. Nebuchadrezzar left only an unorganized peasantry of the country districts. Jeremiah was given permission to choose his own fate (40: 1-6). He chose to stay with Gedaliah, the newly appointed royal governor over the scattered peasantry that had outlived the dangers of the recent years. Gedaliah seems to have been a choice man. Doubtless Jeremiah hoped to strengthen his hand.

8. The Seventh-Century Prophets as Compared with the Eighth-Century Group.

This second prophetic half-century was not as startling a period in point of religious readjustments as the first one, yet it ranks high in the list of important periods of history. Of its five prophets, Zephaniah, Nahum, Jeremiah, Habakkuk, and Ezekiel, each one stands out with clear individuality. They maintain the familiar ideas of God's moral demands, of Judah's varied wickedness, of His certain judgments and of Israel's assured but distant future. Zephaniah and Jeremiah mention the "remnant," while the latter prophet uses the term "Branch" instead of "shoot," when he refers to the anticipated ruler of the "remnant."

These prophets took a wide-ranging view of the Divine power. Jehovah was going to deal summarily with all nations. Habakkuk expressed a rather remarkable philosophy of religion in his explanation of the permanence of righteousness. Yet the three supremely great additions to religious thinking which characterize this age seemed to come out of the experience of Jeremiah. The first of these was a deeper sense of the nature of sin, as something for which each one is responsible (4:4; 17:9), which hardens the heart (7: 24; 9: 14) and creates a barrier between man and God. Again Jeremiah realized, as few before him, the fellowship of man with God. Finally he was led up to the great conception of individualism in religion. Thus religion became something deeper, more personal, more definitely involving individual responsibility, not a mere community or national duty. Ezekiel may have received this last idea from Jeremiah, but he restated it in a very clear form.

[1] Some students make this post-exilic. Compare Nehemiah 13: 19-27. But Deuteronomy 5: 12-15 justifies it.

VII - The Great Prophet of the Early Exile - Ezekiel (586-570 B. C.)

The thorough measures taken by Nebuchadrezzar to make another rebellion in Judah unlikely had the effect of reducing every Jew who was in any respect a leader to apathy or despair. The status of the people seemed hopeless. Those left in Palestine were peasantry of little account. Those carried off to Babylon to be added to the large number already there were broken-hearted. Many had fled to Egypt during the years preceding the great disaster; others were ready to make that venture. To bring these groups of disillusioned, disheartened people into a frame of mind which would permit them to profit by their new environment and to look forward, with as much patience as possible, to better days was a true prophetic task to which Ezekiel set himself in Babylonia. Jeremiah desired to play just such a part in Judah itself. But when Gedaliah, the governor, was slain, the panic-stricken remnant, fearing the blind vengeance of Nebuchadrezzar, fled hastily to Egypt, taking Jeremiah with them. There the great prophet ended his days.

1. The Last Experiences and Sermons of Jeremiah (586 to c. 580 B. C.).

Gedaliah, appointed governor at Mizpah by Nebuchadrezzar, murdered by Ishmael. Jeremiah 40: 7-41: 18.

Jeremiah's vain plea to those who wished to flee to Egypt from Nebuchadrezzar's wrath. 42: 1-43: 7.

His prediction at Tahpanhes of Nebuchadrezzar's certain conquest of Egypt. 43:8-13.

His vain denunciation of the idolatrous worship of Ishtar by his countrymen in Egypt. 44.

2. Ezekiel's Pastoral Messages of Comfort and Hope to the Discouraged Exiles (585-575 B. C.).

The downfall of Jerusalem with its startling confirmation of what Ezekiel had been proclaiming to the exiles, not only gave him fresh prestige, but altered the character of his messages. He ceased to denounce and began to comfort, encourage and inspire. He was no longer the severe critic, but the tender and thoughtful pastor.

The personal responsibility of the prophet for his people and of each Judean for himself. Ezekiel 33: 1-20.

Notwithstanding Jerusalem's fall, those left in the land, if they persist in sinning, will be overtaken by judgment. 33: 21-33.

The neglectful rulers of the past will be replaced under Jehovah, the good guardian Shepherd, by a true Davidic ruler who will give them protection and peace. 34.

Israel's eventual repossession of her own land, cleansed and repopulated, will glorify Jehovah's name in the world. 35, 36.

The vision of the valley of dry bones: Jehovah is able to create the nation anew. 37: 1-14.

The vision of the two sticks: the future people shall be undivided. 37: 15-28.

When the hostile, heathen powers gather for a final, destructive attack on His loyal and happy people, they shall suddenly be destroyed by God Himself. 38, 39.

During the first decade of the exile Ezekiel evidently labored unceasingly to re-establish the morale of his people. It is interesting to note how he seeks to base their confidence upon a fresh sense of Jehovah's power and goodwill. There was no need for despair, while He was active. He could create a living army out of dried-up bones (37). His power was ample to meet any crisis (39). The calamities of the people had been disciplinary; they need not be permanent.

3. Ezekiel's Wonderful Forecast of the Properly Reorganized Holy Land (572 B. C.).

Ezekiel's last prophecy was his greatest one. Ostensibly it was a ground plan of the new temple and state. In fact, it was a bold, original, elaborated scheme of reorganized worship, a true sermon on holy living under the guise of an architect's specifications.

Ezekiel believed that one great source of past failures had been the lack of proper organization in religious practice. Trained in priestly ideas, he believed that a regulation of social and religious methods would be one way of preventing such errors. He wanted to make it reasonably easy for his people to be holy. So he put forth this vision of the temple and of the state that ought to be.

The new temple on Mt. Zion (exclusively) with its gateways, courts, sanctuary, adjuncts, buildings, and altar. Ezekiel 40-43.

The temple officials and life: Levites and priests, the prince, the festivals and the offerings. 44-46.

The life-giving stream flowing out of the heart of the temple, beautifying and redeeming the whole land. 47: 1-12.

The boundaries of this land and the allotments to people and leaders. 47: 13-48: 29.

The appropriate name of the re-established city. 48: 30-35.

This temple was to occupy Mt. Zion exclusively, not sharing it, as in the past, with interests primarily royal. It was to be the real center of the new life

35

of the land. It was to be in sole charge of the priesthood, not, as in the past, controlled by the secular ruler. Out of it was to come a healthful, steady flow of ordered, religious experience, correcting, blessing, and making happy the obedient and devout people. The entire temple plan was thus the remarkably stimulating program of a better-ordered community life for the new nation, set free from captivity and returned to Judah.

Like all great forecasts, while it had much value in shaping the future thinking and the future religious practice of the Jewish people, it was never accurately fulfilled. We should remember that it did not need to be literally carried out in full, practical detail. It was really a very bold prophecy. It achieved its real religious purpose, when it suggested, with such forcefulness and clarity, the true type of the future community, the things which that community should set its heart on doing and the spirit in which they should be done. It was really a trumpet call to a more forceful, religiously minded community life.

4. Ezekiel's Contributions to Religious Thinking.

Ezekiel's task was one of spiritual reconstruction. He had to give his disheartened people a fresh grip upon life and a new point of view. Before the downfall of Jerusalem he naturally sought to show the moral and spiritual reasons for that expected calamity, so that it would not overwhelm the people in Babylonia to whom he was ministering. His greatest service, however, was rendered to the enlarged group of exiles in Babylonia.

He deserves recognition for the directness of his message on behalf of the individual Israelite. He places moral and spiritual responsibility where it must, in the long run, belong, upon the man himself. He nobly asserted the freedom of the individual and his responsibility. At the same time, in chapters 40-48, he set forth graphically the correlated values of institutionalism and of organization. Men have to do God's work together, as a community. There must be some rules to go by, unless anarchy or opportunism are to be the measures of achievement.

Ezekiel was a significant leader. He gave his people a fresh grip on life and a new outlook. He helped them to realize the religious value of proper organization. He dignified the current conceptions of both God and man. He played a very important part in creating the new Israel which faced the new age. Of the close of his life there is no trace.

VIII - The High-Water Mark of Prophetic Thinking - The Isaianic Preachers of the Late Exile (540-536 B. C.)

A quarter-century passed by after the latest date reflected by any of the writings of Ezekiel. The great body of exiles had become reconciled to life in Babylonia, had adjusted their habits to its opportunities, had even found these very alluring. Yet some of them eagerly awaited the day when Jeremiah's predictions (25: 11-14; 29: 10-14; 32: 6-44) of the ending of the power of the Chaldean empire and of the return of the Jewish captives to Judah might be realized. These were thrilled by the news which spread all over Asia about 549 B. C. that a new genius of victory, Cyrus, had appeared, at whose approach whole nations were submitting themselves to his will. They could be sure that in due time such a conqueror would attack the Chaldean dynasty at its capital, Babylon, and test its power. In fact, within three years, all Western Asia had tendered allegiance to Cyrus, except the portions closely controlled from Babylon.

The news of the rapid successes gained by Cyrus, because of his prestige, almost without striking a blow, stirred the hearts of the captives in Babylonia. They began to feel sure that Cyrus was God's appointed instrument to bring about their release.

1. Predictions of Babylon's Approaching Fall (After 545 B. C.).

The well-merited, thorough-going overthrow of glorious Babylon by the Medes: a triumphal ode. Isaiah 13: 1-14: 28.

Babylon, the cruel tyrant, is now about to receive her just deserts. Jeremiah 50: 1-51: 58.

The vision of the army successfully invading Babylon a message for oppressed Judah. Isaiah 21: 1-10.

2. Assurances to the Exiled Community that the Omnipotent Jehovah is About to Deliver His People (Isaiah 40-48). About 540 B. C.

At this juncture among the captives was heard the voice of the greatest of Israel's prophets. Who he was and how so wonderful a personality could remain unknown are two of the puzzles of sacred history. His environment was not only beyond question that of the end of the exile, but his only motive for expression was the desire to capitalize the lessons of the long exile in the interest of a new order of procedure in the future for his people. Even the great-visioned Isaiah of 700 B. C. could not have imagined the situation as it came to exist in 540 B. C. Everything leading nations, political problems, Israel's situation had been radically changed, except the character, power, and purpose of Jehovah. The speaker or writer of Isaiah 40-48 was in all human probability a living prophet of the sixth century, gifted and educated like his great predecessor, whose writings or utterances came to be bound up at a much later date with the genuine Isaianic writings, because they interpreted so nobly and clearly, in the light of these new conditions, the ideals which the great Isaiah had cherished. This prophet of the exile was a great interpreter of the historic past no less than a pleader for a future altogether new.

Israel has paid in full for her sins. Let the glad tidings go forth that the end of the exile is at hand. Isaiah 40: 1-11.

The all-powerful, all-knowing, incomparable, unwearying Jehovah assures this. 40: 12-31.

His sovereignty is shown by His shaping of history. 41.

Jehovah chose and equipped Israel to be His SERVANT, appointed to establish justice and to reveal the truth. 42: 1-9.

Let the whole world celebrate Jehovah's redemption of His people. 42: 10-17.

Israel's plight a well-deserved discipline from which He is now ready and able to deliver her. 42: 18-43: 7.

Israel's splendid task is to bear witness to His redemptive goodness. 43: 8-13.

The deliverance, not due to Israel's merits, but to His grace. 43: 14-28.

It will cause non-Israelites to enrol themselves among His people. 44: 1-5.

In view of Jehovah's uniqueness how foolish idolatry seems! 44: 6-23.

Jehovah, God of creation and prophecy, will grant victory and riches to His anointed, thus giving salvation to the world. 44: 24-45: 25.

Chaldea's hand-made gods are borne here and there, but Jehovah always carries His people. 46.

Babylon, the haughty, luxurious mistress of kingdoms, in spite of her magic and her wise men, is about to be shamefully overthrown. 47.

The crowning proof of Jehovah's greatness and goodness is about to take place; notwithstanding Israel's obstinate sinfulness, the Eternal is about to deliver her. 48.

3. The Fall of Babylon and Friendly Attitude of Cyrus (539 B. C.).

After having completed the conquest of other parts of Asia, Cyrus was at last ready, in 539 B. C., to conquer the Chaldean territories, and thus to make himself the supreme arbiter of the destinies of the active world of that day. The process was brief. He advanced against Babylon, the capital city. Internal treachery on the part of those who despised and hated Nabuna'id, the last Chaldean sovereign, opened the gates to Cyrus, who received a hearty welcome from many more than those who had the status of captives.

For the next thousand years the ruling Influence in Western Asia was Aryan rather than Semitic.

Cyrus was a great ruler, who could deal with peoples fairly. He justified the hopes of those who had so eagerly anticipated his coming by letting them understand that he would place no obstacles in the way of their return to their homes.

4. The Great Glory and the Wonderful Task to be Zion's Through Her Sacrifice and Suffering (Isaiah 49-55). About 538 B. C.

In these remarkable chapters the arguments which prepared the captives to expect the downfall of Babylon no longer appear. Instead the prophet faces the future in a very noble way. An appropriate date seems to be the time immediately succeeding the capture of the city. The three great themes are the mission of the "Servant" and its method, the reunion of Zion with Jehovah her husband, and her glorious future.

The prophet uses two beautiful figures of speech, each meaning the Israel which was to carry out Jehovah's plans, the "remnant," that Israel of the spirit which in truth would respond to Jehovah's loving discipline and would devote itself to His purposes. One of these is the "Servant," which is ideal Israel, thought of as Jehovah's instrument in restoring the unity and prosperity of the nation and in extending the knowledge of Jehovah over the world. The other figure is Zion, not just the city, but the community, now penitent and humbled, but about to receive great blessings and much glory.

The great missionary task for which Jehovah has prepared the SERVANT. Isaiah 49: 1-6.

Abhorred Israel shall be honored; her exiles shall return. 49: 7-13. Zion shall speedily be repopulated and rebuilt. 49: 14-21.

At the powerful word of Jehovah still Israel's husband the nations shall solicitously return her home. 49: 22-50: 3.

The vigilant, docile SERVANT will endure his bitter experiences, relying on Jehovah. 50: 4-11.

Let Jehovah's true-hearted followers take courage. He is behind them. 51: 1-16.

O humiliated Jerusalem, prepare to welcome Him joyfully with the exiles from Babylon. 51: 17-52: 12.

The SERVANT, whose unparalleled and undeserved sufferings open the way for the redemption and forgiveness of the heathen world, shall be gloriously exalted. 52: 13-53: 12.

Zion, now desolate, shall be populous, radiantly beautiful, prosperous and secure. 54.

Let every one be eager to share in the covenant blessings which Jehovah has in store the fulfilment of His plans is at hand. 55.

5. The Commanding Ideas of This Prophetic Thinker.

Just as Ezekiel enabled the disheartened exiles to get a fresh grip on life and made them settle down for a generation, so this great unnamed prophet not only announced their coming freedom, but assigned to it a task at once inspiring and unique. To convert their despairing acquiescence into alert, earnest hopefulness demanded nothing less than a miracle. It required an assurance that the exile was at an end, but much more.

The convincing declarations in regard to the end of the exile were set forth in chapters 40-48. These predictions asserted the victorious career of Cyrus, his appointment of Jehovah's agent, the certain fall of Babylon, Jehovah's readiness to take action, the absurdity of pitting idols against Him, and the sure return of the exiles to Judah.

In chapters 49-55 are set forth the greater plans of which those mentioned were only anticipatory. Israel is God's Servant; her mission is to bring all peoples to Him; her true missionary career is now to begin.

Thinking of these prophecies as a whole (40-55), five great ideas stand out: (1) Jehovah is incomparable, the one and only God, whose purposes can only be understood by one who reviews history and appreciates its moral values; (2) He chose Israel to be His agent in saving the whole world; (3) this agent is not the Israel by birth, but Israel the "remnant," the sum-total of godly Israelites, purified by suffering and discipline, eager for service; (4) this new Israel is to have a great missionary program: her task is to bring all people to the feet of Jehovah, not by force, not merely by proclamation, but by the exhibit of godlike character; (5) Israel's home base, Judah and Jerusalem, joyful, prosperous, blessed in every way, will be a center of light for the world. It is difficult to imagine a more satisfying statement of real religion in the sixth century B. C. In these chapters, for the first time in history, the missionary ideal is stated in universal terms. It marks the highest possible level of religious thought.

IX - The Two Prophets of the Building of The Second Temple - Haggai & Zechariah (520-516 B. C.)

It is one of the paradoxes of history, no less than an illuminating exhibit of human nature, that, when Cyrus gave permission to the Jews to leave Chaldea and to return to Judah, carrying with them their sacred vessels, in order to set up once more their old religious life at the old home, the great majority of them had no desire to return. They preferred the opportunities of the larger world of which they had become a part to the restrictions and privations of Judah and Jerusalem, then more or less in a state of ruin. They preferred the world of business opportunity to that of agriculture. They may have seemed selfish in this choice. The great prophet may have been bitterly disappointed at their attitude. Yet this very reluctance fitted into the Divine plans. The greater part of Judaism became peripatetic. Jews penetrated everywhere, yet remained good Jews. Unconsciously they became, in their way, evangelists of a higher type of faith.

Some did return. The precise number and occasion are matters of discussion. The book of Ezra states that a good-sized delegation returned to Judah promptly, about 536 B. C., rebuilt the altar on the old Temple site, inaugurated a regular service and began to build the second Temple, but that, by the interference of jealous enemies, the work was blocked for fifteen years. Other writers seem to imply a failure to act at all. In any case the returned exiles who were in Judah about 520 B. C. were stirred to enthusiasm in regard to the immediate building of the Temple by two prophets, Haggai and Zechariah, who urged them and their leaders, Zerubbabel, the prince, and Joshua, the high priest, to begin work at once.

1. The Contrasting Personalities of the Two Prophets, Haggai and Zechariah.

Two more diverse men could hardly be imagined, yet each was a real leader of men. Haggai was business-like, yet clever; Zechariah was a scholar with all the resources of a trained intellect, as graphic in his methods as Ezekiel. He could put his pleas into the form of visions for others to interpret. Haggai was more direct, yet he was not destitute of imagination. They made a remarkably efficient pair of religious leaders.

2. Their Repeated Appeals to the Community to Build the Temple.

The Jewish community seems to have become apathetic. Perhaps the distressing contrast between the glowing predictions of the great unknown prophet of Babylon and the sober realities of life in Judah had made them cynical and selfish. In their struggle to maintain themselves they had gradually forgotten all other obligations. Their awakening to duty and to opportunity required the veritable bombardment which they certainly received. Within four months the two prophets made six fervid appeals to the people to do their duty.

September 1, 520 B. C. by Haggai: "Reflect on the explanation of your disappointed hopes; then arise and build." Haggai 1: 1-11.

September 24, by Haggai: "Remember that Jehovah is with you in this enterprise." Haggai 1: 12-15.

October 21, by Haggai: "To this temple, so unpretentious and unattractive in the eyes of some of you, will flow the riches of all nations, so that it will be very glorious." Haggai 2: 1-9.

November, by Zechariah: "Be not like your stubborn fathers. They did evil and were punished." Zechariah 1: 1-6.

December 24, by Haggai: "The priests declare that uncleanness is more infectious than holiness. Rebuild the temple, that with increased holiness may come fresh prosperity." Haggai 2: 10-19.

December 24, by Haggai: "O Zerubbabel, Persia will be overthrown. In that day you shall be Jehovah's viceregent." Haggai 2: 20-23.

Haggai was certainly specific in his expectation of a breaking up of the Persian empire and of the reign of Zerubbabel, who was the living Davidic "shoot" or "branch."

3. The Eight Visions of Zechariah Concerning the Community (Beginning February, 519 B. C.).

These visions were really powerful sermons, either bringing a message of comfort or of hope, or indicating the moral standards which should be upheld in the community of Jehovah's people.

The mounted messengers who report that the world is at peace. "This does not mean a deathblow to all hope. Jehovah loves Zion dearly. He will keep all His promises." Zechariah 1: 7-17.

The four horns representing world powers. "A blacksmith stands ready to crush each one." 1: 18-21.

The surveyor with the measuring line. "Why survey Jerusalem? Jehovah will defend the city which will overspread any walls." 2: 1-5.

The high priest, Joshua, confirmed in his priesthood, purified and honored. "Jehovah confirms your authority, O Joshua, as an earnest of our expectation of the BRANCH. (Compare Isaiah 11: 1; Jeremiah 23: 5; 33: 15.) 3: 1-11.

The golden seven-branched candelabrum flanked by the two guardian olive trees. "Jehovah is on the watch through His representatives. Scoffers will rejoice when Zerubbabel sets the capstone of the Temple." 4: 1-5, 6a, 10b-14, 6b-10a.

The flying roll of parchment, searching out evil-doers. "Jehovah's curse shall be efficient against thieves and perjurers." 5:1-4.

The woman in the large jar. "She is Madame Wickedness, to be carried off to Chaldea, where she belongs." 5: 5-11.

The four war chariots of Jehovah. "Divine justice will be satisfied by a judgment upon the north country." 6: 1-8.

Three of these, the first, second, and eighth, dealt with the relations of the Jewish community to the outside world, declaring that Jehovah was able to cope with any situation. Three others, the third, sixth, and seventh, dealt with the security, size, and moral conditions of the community under Divine guardianship. The remaining two, the fourth and fifth, expressed the sense of hopefulness due to the re-assumption by the community of its religious privileges and obligations. To conceive of a series of prophetic sermons, more definite, more stirring, more suited to the situation would be difficult. Zechariah was a true coadjutor of the great Unknown, who may have been a resident of the Jerusalem community, since there is evidence that Isaiah 60-62 was written in Palestine. Some students would place Isaiah 49-55 in Palestine.

4. Zechariah's Later Prophetic Utterances (About 519-517 B. C.).

These wonderful visions, which were probably put forth from time to time during a period of some months following February, 519, gave Zechariah a clear place as the trusted adviser of the community and made him widely known. At some later date, perhaps within 519, a deputation of four men came from Babylon to Jerusalem with gifts, which, doubtless, were to help in completing the Temple. This gave the prophet another opportunity to honor Zerubbabel as the civil head of the community and the focus of Jewish hopes.

The golden crown for Zerubbabel. "Make a crown from the golden gift from Babylon, place it on the head of Zerubbabel, the BRANCH, who will build the Temple and rule with Joshua as his coadjutor." [1] Zechariah 6: 9-15.

The reply to the deputation from Bethel which inquired about the necessity of maintaining the fasts in memory of the destruction of Jerusalem and the Temple (December 4, 518 B. C.).

"Did you fast in order to express repentance? Your own experience and the teaching of the prophets have taught that what Jehovah really desires are deeds of brotherliness, justice and mercy." Zechariah 7: 1-14.

Ten predictions regarding the Jerusalem-to-be. (1) Dearly loved by Jehovah (vs. 1, 2); (2) A faithful city (v. 3); (3) A community of safe, happy homes (vs. 4, 5); (4) An achievement wholly possible for Jehovah (v. 6); (5) A city to whose security Jehovah will bring back the exiles (vs. 7, 8); (6) A community very prosperous (vs. 9-13); (7) A righteously acting community (vs. 14-17); (8) Which turns fasts into holidays (vs. 18, 19); (9) Attracting peoples who will visit Jerusalem to gain a blessing (vs. 20-22); (10) Peoples of various tongues will desire to become Jews and followers of Jehovah (v. 23). Zechariah 8.

These declarations reach a very high level ethically and spiritually. Their value in the readjustment of religious standards and practice in the Judean community must have been very great.

5. The Apocalyptical Element in Prophecy.

With Haggai and Zechariah appears a growing phase of prophecy destined in time to supplant true prophecy altogether. This phase found its earliest expression in Zephaniah's declaration, about a century before, that Jehovah (Zephaniah 3: 8) would assemble the nations for judgment, thus giving the righteous "remnant" a chance. Ezekiel (chs. 38, 39) even more explicitly looked forward to a sweeping judgment of Jehovah which would eventually dispose of hostile peoples and enable Him to fulfil His promises. This anticipation of a future putting forth of almighty power was nourished by the political helplessness of the Jews. No other way of bringing true Israel to the leadership of the world seemed possible. It really, however, placed a limitation upon God's power and assumed that His purposes were only to be fulfilled materially. As a matter of fact, these prophets were unable to grasp at the time God's real way of fulfilling prophecy. Haggai and Zechariah seem to have been confident that God would speedily open the way for Zerubbabel to be the fulfiller of the Messianic hopes expressed since Isaiah's time. It seems very clear, one may say in all reverence, that in this respect they went beyond what Jehovah had revealed to them. Their God-given task was to build the Temple, and to reconstruct the community. It seemed to them that the next step must be the realization of dynastic hopes in Zerubbabel; but this turned out not to be a part of God's plan.

Other peculiarities of sixth-century prophecy are noteworthy. Zechariah, like Ezekiel, revelled in the use of symbolism. This may have been due in part to the Chaldean environment, with which both were familiar; and in part to the danger of being too explicit. Zechariah, too, makes use of angelic intermediaries between Jehovah and His people. Angelology in the Bible is clearly due in part to the influence of Persia upon Hebrew thinking. In a growing degree Jehovah became aloof, supreme in majesty. The thought of fellowship with Him, stressed by Jeremiah, receded, to be kept alive by psalmists, until reasserted by Jesus.

Prophecy, therefore, was already unconsciously working away from the splendid idealism of Isaiah 40-55, under the spell of the enthusiasm aroused by the thought of community restoration and prosperity. Israel's glory rather than Israel's task occupied the hearts of the religiously minded. A trend of thinking developed which was never set straight, until Jesus recalled to his disciples the essential teachings of the spiritually minded prophets.

6. The Completion and Dedication of the Second Temple (Ezra 5, 6). 516 B. C.

Under the competent leadership of Haggai, Zechariah, Zerubbabel, and Joshua, the Temple was pushed to completion, in spite of all manner of delays and difficulties, in 516 B. C. The writer of Ezra implies that the sanction of the great Darius himself was eventually obtained for the enterprise. The successful outcome was mainly due, however, to the earnest and diligent service of the people, who rejoiced greatly over the completion of the project. Haggai did not err in asserting the significance of this Temple, modest as it must have been in comparison to the former one. It quickly became the working center of Judaism, the symbol of everything important in Jewish life.

[1] For the necessary readjustment of verses 11-13, consult a good commentary.

X - The Prophets of Community Reform Just Preceding Nehemiah (About 450 B. C.)

More than half a century, spanning the remainder of the long reign of Darius the Great (521-485 B. C.), the reign of his son, Xerxes I (486-466 B. C.), and a portion of the reign of Artaxerxes I (466-425 B. C.), seems to have passed before another period of prophetic activity was reached. Why this was so we may only conjecture. On the one hand, the completion of the Temple was an achievement so notable as to satisfy. The prophets had set forth the methods and spirit which it was to inaugurate and the ends it would help to accomplish. Naturally they would wait to see what would happen. On the other hand, the dynastic hopes which had rested on Zerubbabel were gradually disappointed. Just as soon as Darius felt himself firmly settled on his imperial throne, he reorganized the empire in accordance with a new system. In place of the native leadership recognized by Cyrus, Darius appointed governors wholly unrelated to the people governed. This policy probably accounted for the unrecorded disappearance of Zerubbabel and his descendants. They never had a chance to rule Judah.

For some reason not clearly known the Judean community gradually became more or less demoralized. It kept up the formal worship at the Temple, but slackened in its enthusiasm. A spirit of greed and selfishness prevailed, a very natural accompaniment of discouragement. All this is reflected in Isaiah 56-59, 63-66, and in Malachi. Since each of these refers to Edom's recent calamity, which is likewise the theme of Obadiah, the three are grouped as prophetic sermons of the years immediately preceding the reform of Ezra and Nehemiah. Isaiah 60-62 may belong to the period immediately following the completion of the Temple.

1. The Great Unknown's Last Vision Regarding Jerusalem (Isaiah 60-62; 19:18-25). About 500 B. C.

These three chapters are very much like chapters 40-55, yet they seem quite certainly to have been written in Jerusalem after the completion of the Temple (60: 7) and before Nehemiah's day (60: 10).

The glories of restored Jerusalem. Isaiah 60.
The many-sided task of the true prophet. 61: 1-4.
Jehovah's people shall be the privileged among nations. 61: 5-11.
Righteous, triumphant Israel shall be Jehovah's delight, protected from despoiling. 62: 1-9.
Let all exiles return, so that Zion shall be recognized and honored. 62: 10-12.
The great political and religious transformation which the world will see. 19: 18-25.

These beautiful expressions of the joyousness, glory, and greatness of the task awaiting Jehovah's people, its many-sidedness, its blessedness, brilliance and universal range represent again the loftiest height of Old Testament aspiration. Intelligent, generous, sacrificial, spiritual world service was a far greater ideal than social justice and community brotherhood.

2. Isaianic Messages of Condemnation, Promise, and Exhortation to the Judean Community (Isaiah 56-59, 63-66). About 460 B. C.

Those who practise righteousness, even eunuchs and foreigners, shall have full Temple rights. Isaiah 56: 1-8.
The gluttonous, drunken rulers of the community and those who practise heathenish ways Jehovah must punish. 56: 9-57: 13.

To the humble and contrite the Holy One brings comfort, peace, and fellowship. 57: 14-21.

True Temple worship is not a perfunctory observance of forms, but genuinely righteous procedure. 58.

With the crimes of the community which hinder its salvation Jehovah will resolutely deal. 59.

The "day" of His triumphant vengeance over His foes is at hand. 68: 1-6.

"Just as thou, O Jehovah, didst lovingly deliver thy people in the past, so intervene again for us, unworthy as we are." 63: 7 - 64: 12.

The half-heathen in the community will incur Jehovah's righteous judgment: the faithful and loyal He will vindicate and bless. 65, 66.

A careful reading shows that these chapters neither mention a deliverance, like chapters 40-48, nor do they refer to Israel's world mission, like chapters 49-55. They deal with community reform in loyalty to the great ideals of the past, a noble theme, yet quite distinct from those which occupied the forefront of prophetic thinking in the exile.

3. The Vision of Obadiah Regarding Edom (Obadiah). 460-450 B. C.

This short prophetic outburst must, on its face, be later than 586 B. C., the date of Jerusalem's destruction (v. 11). As a whole it reflects some great disaster which has come upon the Edomites, over which the prophet expresses satisfaction. This disaster was probably their expulsion from Petra, their home, by the Nabatseans, at about the middle of the fifth century B.C.

Word comes that other nations have combined against Edom. Obadiah, v. 1.

That proud, self-sufficient people Jehovah easily can humble. vs. 2-4.

O Edom, your trusted allies have driven you out, despite your wise men and warriors, vs. 5-9.

This has happened in recompense for your aloofness and cruelty in the day of Judah's distress, vs. 10-14.

In the day of Jehovah's judgment Israel will in her turn destroy Edom according to her deserts and once more possess her own ancestral land. vs. 15-21.

As in the case of the paean of Nahum, this shout of joy over the rumored destruction of a people is to be interpreted as due to the thought of the removal of an obstruction to Israel's future, not to a spirit of malignancy.

4. Malachi's Appeal for a True Community Reform (Malachi). About 450-440 B. C.

The book of Malachi is really anonymous. The name may be merely descriptive. It means "my messenger." The low moral and spiritual tone of the community, the lack of zeal for the proper management of the Temple service, and the prevalence of a spirit of skepticism and discouragement, which these prophecies reflect, are the very evils which Nehemiah and Ezra aimed to reform. Hence Malachi is probably to be dated not long before 444 B. C., the generally accepted date of the thorough-going movement for reform which resulted in the adoption of the Law as presented by the scribal movement, and in the establishment of Judaism as the regulatory system of social and religious life. The opening reference to Edom's disaster alludes, in all probability, to the expulsion of that people by the Nabataeans, referred to above. The community was ruled by a Persian governor (1:8).

Superscription by the editor. Malachi 1:1.

Jehovah's attitude toward Edom only goes to prove His discriminating love for Jacob. 1: 2-5.

Yet the priesthood of the Temple dishonor Him, daring to offer blemished sacrifices, regarding their duties as wearisome, wholly unworthy of their great heritage. 1: 6-2: 9.

Moreover the people profane their covenant with Jehovah by divorcing their Jewish wives in order to marry foreign-born women. 2: 10-16.

Jehovah's purifying judgment will come suddenly to cleanse the priesthood and all evil-doers. 2: 17-3: 6.

Only the conscientious paying of what is due Him will bring His blessing. 3: 7-12.

The DAY is coming when the godless and the faithful shall alike be dealt with suitably. 3: 13-4: 3.

Obey the (Deuteronomic) Law. A second Elijah will come to set right all social discord. 4: 4-6.

5. The Leading Ideas of the Fifth Century.

A growing spirit of legalism is reflected in the declarations of this age. In the Isaianic chapters and in Malachi may be noted frequent references to ritual observances and to temple worship. Another prominent theme is the presence in the community of outsiders. Malachi lays stress upon racial purity and reserve. But these prophets were more than formalists. They are concerned about the spirit which undergirds and expresses all observances. They assert real moral and spiritual values in the old-fashioned prophetic way. It is easy to see how truly they prepared the way for the sweeping reforms of Ezra and Nehemiah.

6. The Establishment of Judaism (About 444 B. C.).

In the books of Ezra and Nehemiah is to be found the Chronicler's account of the rehabilitation of the community and city under Nehemiah's masterly leadership and of the propounding and adoption of the Levitical Law under the joint auspices of Ezra, the scribe, and Nehemiah, the governor. The building of the wall, the reorganization of the community, and the achievement of security made the people, more tender of conscience because of the faithful preaching of these prophets, ready for a fresh religious start. Judaism began with the solemn adoption of the Law as edited by the scribal order. It meant a considerable readjustment of life. It was a great social and religious venture, which has functioned to the present day.

XI - Prophetic-Apocalyptic Voices of Later Times

The remaining prophetic passages of the Old Testament were increasingly apocalyptic in their trend. Religious leaders seemed to be dreaming of a great miraculous destructive interposition by Jehovah which would make it possible for Israel to do her part in the world. Such thoughts tended to obscure the true missionary idealism of the exile. They encouraged the people to wait for Jehovah to act, instead of doing what was within their own power.

The actual dates of these utterances are rather uncertain.

1. An Isaianic Vision of Vengeance and Blessing (Isaiah 34, 35).

Jehovah's judgment is sure to fall upon hostile nations, especially upon Edom. Isaiah 34: 1-17.

A joyous, beautiful and safe future shall then follow for Jehovah's people. 35.

These sharply contrasted pictures of catastrophic judgment and wholesale vengeance, to be recorded and fulfilled to the letter (34: 16, 17), and of the happy, healthy, fertile life of the godly minded are characteristically apocalyptic.

2. Joel's Announcement of Jehovah's Day of Judgment (Joel 1-3). About 375 B. C.

The three principal reasons for dating Joel in the early part of the fourth century are the natural references to the small Judean community, to the Temple and to a walled city, the references to the Greeks (3: 6) and the apocalyptical view-point.

Superscription. Joel 1:1.

The unprecedented locust plague has caused widespread distress. 1: 2-12.

Summon the community to a penitential assembly because of the terrible visitation. 1: 13-20.

Sound the alarm: the locust army is a harbinger of Jehovah's DAY. 2:1-11.

Even now a public repentance may avail to turn aside the Divine wrath. 2: 12-17.

Jehovah replies to the repentant people: The locusts shall perish and the land shall again rejoice. 2: 18-27.

On the new DAY the whole community shall have the prophetic gift. 2: 28-32.

The nations which have oppressed Judah shall be judged by Jehovah. 3: 1-8.

Let these nations appear to meet their doom. 3: 9-17.
Judah shall enjoy every coveted blessing. 3: 18-21.

Joel registers two very distinct advances in religious thinking of differing merit. He sets forth the great idea that in course of time every one, high or low, will be the channel of Divine influence. He likewise explicitly declares Jehovah's judgment would be a sweeping one against "the nations."

3. The Parable of Jonah: A Protest Against Judaism's Anti-missionary Spirit (Jonah 1-4). About 300 B. C.

The book of Jonah is clearly a parable. It is full of improbabilities; yet it was a marvellously great sermon to the narrow-minded Jews who desired to have the nations destroyed and were not very anxious to have them repent and be forgiven. It reaches the highest spiritual levels of the Old Testament. Such a noble picture of Divine love for the world proves that apocalyptic emphasis was, after all, only one phase of later Jewish religious thought, and that a true missionary idealism had its advocates.

Jonah vainly tries to evade the mission to which God appointed him. Jonah 1: 1-2: 10.

The people of Nineveh repent at his preaching and are forgiven. 3. The unhappy intolerance of the prophet God rebukes by declaring

His unlimited love for the repentant world. 4.

4. Prophetic Stories About Daniel and His Friends (Daniel i, 3-6). Third Century B. C.

The story form was often used in Hebrew and Jewish days to convey needed lessons of life. Ruth, Esther, Jonah, Tobit, Judith, and the group of stories regarding Joseph are illustrative of this. The Daniel stories probably passed from mouth to mouth much earlier than the well-established date of the book of Daniel as a whole. Their inaccuracies regarding the events of the exile make it certain that the knowledge regarding those days was traditional. Their value is not that of careful history, but of stories which had the power to inspire and sustain Jewish courage in the late Greek period, when it was given so severe a testing.

How God rewarded the fidelity to the Law of the four Jewish captives. Daniel 1.
How He delivered from death the three who refused to apostatize. 3.
How He humbled the mighty Nebuchadrezzar because of his pride. 4.
How Belshazzar's act of sacrilege was punished. 5.
How Daniel, condemned to death for his religious faithfulness, was preserved alive hi the den of lions. 6.

These stories assume that the truly righteous man is one who strictly follows the precepts of Judaism. They nobly uphold religious faithfulness, the scorn of personal consequences, the value of exact obedience, God's support of devotedness, His supremacy above all earthly might or majesty, the seriousness of any profanation of His holiness. Their value in the dreadful days of Antiochus Epiphanes was beyond expression.

5. An Apocalyptic Vision of World Judgment (Isaiah 24-27).

The date of these chapters is uncertain. Students incline to date them about the time of the victorious advance of Alexander the Great into Asia (330 B. C.) or later.

Jehovah's destructive judgment is about to fall on all classes. His enemies shall be trodden into the dust. Isaiah 24, 25.
His own people may rely on His protection. 26: 1-27: 1.
Israel is His vineyard: His dealings with His people will be friendly. 27: 2-11.
Those who have been lost will be restored. 27: 12, 13.

Another instructive and characteristic apocalypse in which lyrical outbursts which rejoice over worldwide catastrophe (24:3, 13, 19, 20), the downfall of some foreign city (25: 1-5) and the crushing of Moab (25: 9-12) alternate with tender, catholic presentations of Jehovah's goodness (25: 6-8; 26: 1-7).

6. The Vision of a Judaized World Empire Ruled from Jerusalem by the Prince of Peace (Zechariah 9-14).

These chapters reflect another world than chapters 1-8. The foes are Greeks, no longer distant slave traders as in Joel, but dangerous foes close at hand.

The conquest of Israel's foes and the setting up of the Messianic Kingdom. Zechariah 9.
Jehovah, as guardian and leader, will restore His scattered people. 10.
Judah's traitorous rulers will meet a well-deserved fate. 11; 13: 7-9.
Jerusalem shall be delivered from hostile attack for a glorious future, 12: 1-13: 6; 14.

These chapters clearly reflect the struggle of Judaism with Hellenism. The Jews are world-dwellers. There is a sharp cleavage within Jewish ranks. The times are stormy and distressing. The final chapter is possibly the last word of Biblical apocalypse. Its picture of the future is very characteristic and not at all of a missionary tone.

7. The Substitution of Apocalypse for Prophecy.

The next real prophet of Jewish history was John the Baptist, who recalled the minds of his generation both to the appearance of the early prophets and to their stirring ethical and spiritual messages. He was recognized at once as a genuine prophet. During the intervening two centuries there had been no lack of religious leadership, but it was all apocalyptic in temper. It despaired of converting the world to God; it waited for Him to put forth His power; it was passive rather than active. Yet apocalypse fulfilled an important function. It was prolific. The books of Daniel and of Enoch were followed by many volumes of large circulation. These writers kept alive a confidence in God and His purposes; they reinforced Jewish loyalty to Him; they turned all hopes to the Messiah. Despite the occasional puerility of their conceptions and their overemphasis of the catastrophic method which God would adopt, they subserved a useful purpose. We may be grateful, however, that in the person of our Lord there arose an interpreter through whose sane, illuminative, simple declarations regarding God, life, and service, the real spirit of the prophets once more spoke to men with a fullness and finality that made the prophets of to-day those who are most faithful in interpreting his messages.

XII - A General Review of Hebrew Prophecy

The preceding chapters have directed the attention of the student to four matters: (1) the proper organization chronologically of the prophetic material; (2) the personality of each prophet, so far as known; (3) their actual messages, recorded by them or by others; and (4) the contribution of each prophetic period to the thinking of the world about God and life. It now remains to gather up these and other values more carefully.

1. The Centuries of Prophetic Activity.

The prophets were a recognized factor in the life of the Hebrew people from the days of Samuel and David, when they first attained some measure of public recognition, to the Greek period or even later, when there still arose occasionally a prophetic voice to express God's care for his repentant children, as well as His wrath upon the disobedient and the stubborn. For seven or eight centuries the prophetic order was to be reckoned with as a shaping influence over life and thought. Of these centuries the most important were clearly the eighth, seventh, and sixth.

2. The Character of That Activity.

A prophet filled a large and important place in the community and state. The members of the order had many functions. They were preachers, teachers, personal and public advisers, historiographers, editors. They utilized any method which gave them a chance to bring men into line with God. Some of them wrote histories which were effective sermons; others preached or wrote the powerful appeals which we have studied; still others labored usefully but inconspicuously as good and wise friends of the people. That false prophets were frequent is but a natural corollary of the usefulness and influence of the real prophets.

3. The Natural Groupings of Prophecy.

The Old Testament records show very clearly that while the prophetic order was always a serviceable group in the Israelitish community, there were times of special emergency which called a great leader, like Isaiah, into the forefront. There were also certain distinct eras of such activity when prophetic groups appeared. There were also periods when a group of prophets did a distinctive service for their people. From the days of Samuel to those of Zechariah 9-14 we may distinguish six fairly well defined groups: (1) the prophetic order and its leaders prior to the days of Amos; (2) the four prophets of the latter half of the eighth century: (3) the five prophets of the half -century preceding the exile; (4) the four prophets of the seventy years; (5) the prophets immediately antedating the community reforms of Nehemiah and Ezra; and (6) the prophetic-apocalyptic voices of later days. Each of these groups represents a certain phase of religious experience and is characterized by a distinctive emphasis upon ideas.

4. The Prophetic Personalities.

Some of the prophets have well-defined personalities. They seem like old friends. Their experiences are instructive. They approached the problems of righteous living from every conceivable angle of experience, so that for all time their interpretations of opportunity and of duty are such as stir men to loyalty, faith, and perseverance. Men like Amos, Isaiah, Jeremiah, and Ezekiel were real men, who attacked genuine human problems, which are still the problems of the race. Men need to-day to be brought into the presence of God, to have the Divine point of view made clear regarding their deeds, and to become active instruments of the Divine purpose. These great leaders who embodied in themselves the faith, the courage, and the hopefulness which helped their own generation to face boldly moral and spiritual crises are still inspirers of noble and fruitful living.

5. The Prophetic Teaching About God.

Each prophetic message started from some deep conviction about God, which gave authority and power to what the prophet had to say, and led him to predict how Jehovah would deal with some critical human situation. A conviction of Jehovah's righteousness gave Amos confidence to score the unrighteous daily life of Israel's leaders. It was His loving-kindness that assured Hosea that his people would not be destroyed vindictively but rather disciplined into repentance. It was the thought of the Almighty ruler of the world which gave Isaiah his sense of the unchangeable purpose of God to be surely fulfilled at some future time through the repentant "remnant." It was the sense of Divine fellowship with God that gave Jeremiah courage to stand firm, when his whole world opposed his course. It was the conviction that Jehovah was the Master Providence of the world that gave to Jeremiah and Ezekiel alike the certainty that the downfall of the state was not the end of Jehovah's plans, but only their continuance with fresh force. It was His unrestricted power and goodness that encouraged the unnamed prophet of the exile to predict that its end was sure. Each prophet based his certitude and insight upon his own growing vision of the Divine.

What a characterization of God they came in time to make one who is all-knowing, all-powerful, yet rather to be described in terms of character, perfectly moral, essentially spiritual. Yet their idea of Jehovah gave Him reality. He was a Leader, planning for His people, moulding them by the changing experiences of human life into fit instruments of His holy and persistent purpose for the world. He was a tender Father, infinitely forgiving, yet also wise. Such a picture is wholly without real parallel in literature during or before the prophetic era.

6. The Prophetic View of Social Duty.

The prophets of the two centuries preceding the exile faced a situation which is duplicated every day of the twentieth century. During the exile and ever after, the Jewish community was a church rather than a nation, but from the days of Uzziah and Jeroboam II to those of Zedekiah it was a people with problems which are wholly familiar to people to-day and quite parallel to their own. Wealth and poverty, justice and bad faith, fairmindedness and oppression, goodness and deviltry are conditions which modern communities have to face. These prophets dealt with the evils they saw, just as a preacher of righteousness in any age must do. They declared that a God who was moral demanded that His people should be moral, and that a moral and spiritual breakdown of the people would be firmly taken in hand by Him. Starting in the days of Amos with a strong sense of the collective responsibility of a family or community or state for the acts of its members, the prophets, by the time of Ezekiel, reached the explicit declaration that God holds each normal human being responsible for the right use of his own powers. These social principles are still sound.

A supremely great height of moral and spiritual duty was expressed in Isaiah 40-55. No moral opportunity can be higher than a sacrifice made on behalf of those who are contemptuous, incredulous, or hostile. To be despised and rejected of men is, even to-day, a test of sincerity and courage which few can face. Modern social and political life is often more closely modelled after the standards of the age of the Judges than by those of the prophet of the sixth century B. C. The Old Testament still furnishes an impulse toward repentance and reform for the average man.

7. The Divine Plan in Prophecy.

Real Messianic prophecy began with Isaiah and his declarations regarding the leadership which God would raise up in due time for the "remnant." Of his glorious vision and of those that followed there will be later mention. Far back of this conception lies a broader prophetic idea, wrought into those matchless narratives of Israel's early history which are now an indistinguishable part of the Pentateuch. It is the thought of the Hebrews as a chosen race from the days of their great ancestor, Abraham:

"I will make of thee a great nation,
And I will bless thee and make thy name great.
I will bless them that bless thee,
And him that curse th thee will I curse;
And in thee shall all the families of the earth be blessed."

The prophetic writers of Israel's history made clear His guidance of His people through the trying centuries of growth. They kept their eyes upon a promising future. They accepted disasters as punishments well deserved by a people whose ideals ought to have been loftier and more in accordance with those of their God. His character, His choice of Israel to be His people, the moral and spiritual obligations thus resting upon them, and, particularly, His attitude 'toward the world to which His own people were to be His interpreters and messengers are elements in a prophetic vision of history in the making, which ever kept both prophets and people looking ahead to the certain fulfilment of the Divine plan for the world.

8. The Messianic Idea in Prophecy.

When the prophet Hosea grasped the wonderful truth that Jehovah's greatest attribute was not His power or His righteousness but his unquenchable, unchanging love, he really made the Messianic idea inevitable. Hosea did not give it expression; a greater than he, however, was fortunately at hand. Isaiah's comprehending mind could see that such a God must not only forgive one who was repentant, but must also make provision for his service. Hence Isaiah both proclaimed that there would be a repentant, righteous "remnant" and declared that Jehovah would give this "remnant" a fitting leadership, that it might become His true agent in blessing the world. This leader was to be of the royal Davidic line. He was to deliver his people and reign over them righteously. He was to be a great personality, a refuge for those in need. His task would be to enable his people to rise to the height of their best selves. He and the "remnant" had a common program.

These two ideas, that of a "remnant," really fitted in character and experience to execute God's plans, and that of its needed leader, persist with every later prophet who alluded to the Divine purpose for the world. Jeremiah, Ezekiel, and Zechariah favor the figurative but natural terms, "branch" and "shepherd." The unnamed prophet of the exile used one yet more felicitous, the "servant," a term connoting the significance and method of the tasks of the leader. In his great prophecies the term "servant" seemed to mean both the "remnant" and its leader, united in the great service of world redemption. This ideal transcended the prophetic thinking of later periods. A military and political rather than a spiritual leadership seemed to be that for which they longed, especially as prophecy verged into apocalypse.

9. The Missionary Idea in Prophecy.

The idea that the purified "remnant," the true Israel, God's agent in converting the world, was to be aggressive in this task, taking the message of salvation to the ends of the earth, is one of the climaxes of prophetic thought. One who reviews prophecy before the exile will realize that a true missionary view-point did not exist in the eighth century. Isaiah and Micah dreamed of the world as streaming to Jerusalem to receive instruction regarding God. They did not think of the Hebrews, however devoted, as going out into the world with the good news about God and His ways. Before a real missionary definition of Israel's duty could be formulated, it was necessary that the experience of the people in hopeless exile should teach their leaders that a true religious life was possible apart from Jerusalem or the Temple or its familiar ritual. It was also necessary that they should come to understand that each righteous individual, rather than the nation, was God's working unit for the execution of His plans. A missionary program is only possible after religion becomes portable and individualized, so that any people at any place may, in small groups or even one by one, be brought into the family of God.

10. The Strength and Weakness of Apocalypse.

Prophecy at its best, like preaching, was frank, open, and direct. It sought to influence action, to produce results. It faced all forms of sin and demanded repentance and righteous living. It regarded God's people as chosen by Him in order that they might serve Him intelligently and with devotion, in His desire to win the world to obedience.

The apocalyptical element in prophecy began to appear after Jehovah's people had begun to realize their political insignificance and weakness and the folly of presuming to assume a place of leadership among the nations. It was assumed, wrongly, of course, yet naturally, that the Israel of God would need to acquire a political and social control of the world in order to become its religious leader. Thus Haggai and Zechariah seemed to interpret the glowing promises of Isaiah 40-55, when they predicted an immediate disruption of the Persian empire and the aggrandisement of Zerubbabel. The solution they adopted was that a time would come when Jehovah would sweep away all hostile powers, all opposing agencies, and inaugurate a Messianic era, when His people would have free sway. This came to be the keynote of popular preaching. Its defects were that it encouraged passivity, lost sight of a

55

missionary program, placed all responsibility upon God and emphasized nationalistic hopes. On the other hand, apocalypse kept alive the consciousness of God's power and purpose. Its despair of reaching Divine results by normal methods in this world led it to explore the heavenly world of unseen realities and to dwell upon it as the answer to earthly disappointments. The apocalyptical thinking of the two centuries before Christ became thus a kind of bridge between the religious ideals and aspirations of the preceding centuries and the sane, all-rounded religious thinking of our Lord.

11. The Permanent Contribution of Hebrew Prophecy to Religious Thinking.

Only by such a historical survey as that furthered by these outlines can a proper estimate of Hebrew prophecy be made. One who reverts to the age of Elisha and Uzziah and Jeroboam II realizes how completely the religious life of that day, however genuine, was expressed in ritual observances. Religious habit is important, yet not the most important element in religion. One contribution of supreme importance to true religious thinking was the direct, definite insistence of the prophets of the eighth century upon character as the fundamental element in true religion, the distinctive element in God Himself, the essential expression of the Divine in life. Those were the fundamental assumptions. A third principle of religious life they made a corollary to these. True moral and spiritual character must display itself in the actions and motives of every-day life. Repeatedly the prophets declared that Jehovah could not accept the worship of those whose actions failed to conform to these principles. Another great declaration, made first by Hosea but adopted by all who followed him, emphasized the essential quality of God as love, so that vindictiveness was no trait of His. This was a really great and constructive idea. It was paralleled by the declaration of Micah that Jehovah is essentially reasonable in His demands. The prophets of the next century and of the exile brought out the possible fellowship of God with man and emphasized the creative, world-ruling, sovereign aspects of God. When the great unnamed Isaianic writer had completed his picture of God's power and purpose, the doctrine of God had been set forth in a truly adequate way to the world.

The teaching of the prophets regarding man and his place in the universe was equally fine. While most of the prophets were thinking about Israel as a chosen people, they fairly emphasized the idea that this choice was for service and that it carried moral obligations of a severe character. While every prophet maintained a lofty moral standard, it took a thinker with the freedom and range of an Isaiah 40-55 to crown this service with the missionary ideal for the world.

No less striking is the prophetic conception of the greater world. It is to be estimated by men as God estimates it. Canon Freemantle gained the inspiration for his famous book, "The World as the Subject of Redemption," from the prophets. He adopted their grand idea that the world was to become transformed in good time into the Kingdom of God. This is the conception which unifies all prophetic thinking. The loyal acceptance of Jehovah by all peoples was the great objective before them. The work of the Messiah was only a means to this greater end. It was too great an idea for a prophet of the eighth century B. C. to grasp in all its fullness. Such a thinker could only have a vision of the whole world coming to Jerusalem. The disasters of the seventh century forced Jeremiah and his associates and successors to see that Jerusalem, the Temple, and the nation were not as essential to the working out of the Divine plan as were the purified, obedient "remnant" and their needed leader. Nothing ever caused any prophet to swerve from the belief that eventually the whole world would be Jehovah's. Apocalyptists might feel that the missionary process could not really begin until Jehovah Himself opened the way by rising in His Divine might to destroy the hostile influences, political or social, world-wide or local, which were blocking Israel's progress. Nationalists might emphasize a purely political ambition and forget the religious idealism, yet the underlying thought of God's rule of the whole world was never out of mind.

This great thought is still at the root of all religious progress. The missionary idea redeems society from selfishness, gives it a true impulse toward sound, sane development, and focuses its attention upon God and His world.

12. The Uniqueness of Prophecy.

Hebrew prophecy was unique because the God whose will the prophets sought to express was incomparable. Just as He was not in the class of ordinary national deities, so His true prophets rose above the shrewdness, the canniness, the conventions of a professional group of leaders of community religious and social life. The nearest analogy in modern life to the great prophets of twenty-five centuries or more ago is to be found in the fearless interpreters of the Divine to men, who are found in the pulpit or in public life or in literature. Now, as then, God uses such great persuasive personalities to bring men face to face with moral and spiritual decisions, which shape destinies. They uphold the ideal in the face of terrible pressure to relax its demands; they honor obedience to conscience, notwithstanding the loss of popularity or wealth or ease or even life itself; they believe in the irresistible power of truth and right; they are undiscouraged by reverses or disappointments; they scout the permanence of selfish, brutal, cynical force; they confirm the faith of the world in a future day when God's ways will be those of the whole world. Prophets are still essential in a growing society; they forbid stagnation and cultivate alertness. So long as they exist men will continue to look up and forward, will challenge evil, however entrenched, will value sacrifice as stronger than might, and will fall into line to do their individual share in making the world into the Kingdom of God.

Appendices

I - General Reference Literature for Further Study

This little volume is intended to lay a broad foundation for a lifelong study of Old Testament prophecy. It should not be regarded as a proper substitute for the more thorough treatment to be found in an Old Testament history, in a volume which discusses some phase of prophecy or in a good commentary on any one of the prophetic books. It merely makes a sound and useful introduction to any subsequent studies. Some of the books which may be used to good advantage in such studies are hereinafter mentioned. No attempt is made to make the bibliography complete. Every student, as he or she advances in an understanding of prophecy, will discover books of reference which seem to be of greatest usefulness. A reference library varies to some degree with the individual.

A student of prophecy should plan to own in course of time a good Bible dictionary, a concordance, an atlas, one or two Old Testament histories, some good commentaries, and a good history of Old Testament literature. The suggestions which follow are intended to meet the needs of the average man or woman who desires to acquire a working knowledge of Biblical prophecy for the sake of a better equipment as a teacher.

There are three good Bible dictionaries, each in one volume. That by J. D. Davis (any denominational bookstore) is very condensed, but it answers all questions of fact. The other two are much more extensive and, of course, more costly, yet they are also more illumining. The latest and best is Hastings' One Volume Dictionary of the Bible (Scribner's); the other the Jacobus Standard Bible Dictionary (Funk and Wagnalls), is slightly more conservative in its judgments. There are two concordances which are of handy size, Cruden's and Walker's. The former is sold at a very low price, but is less complete than Walker's Comprehensive Concordance (all religious bookstores). For a large Bible Atlas George Adam Smith's "*Atlas of the Historical Geography of the Holy Land*" is the best available. It is quite expensive. For all practical purposes MacCoun's Atlas (Revell) is sufficient.

There are two reliable and useful Old Testament Histories in one volume, the author's "*History of the Hebrews*" (Scribner's) and "*Old Testament History*," by Professor Ismar J. Peritz (Methodist Book Concern). Professor Kent's "*The Historical Bible*," four volumes covering the Old Testament (Scribner's), covers the same ground in much greater detail. On Old Testament literature, a valuable book to own is Professor Henry T. Fowler's "*A History of the Literature of Ancient Israel*" (Macmillan). A very recent and very valuable volume which reviews the relation of prophecy to national and world problems is Knudson's "*The Prophetic Movement in Israel*" (Meth. Book Concern).

Of commentaries there are many. No series is ever perfectly even. There are two excellent one-volume commentaries on the whole Bible. Dummelow, "*The One Volume Bible Commentary*" (Macmillan), can be commended as truly useful. Peake's "*A Commentary on the Bible*" (Nelson) is, on the whole, the best compact commentary in print. It reflects throughout the historical viewpoint. Whenever a student desires a learned, minutely adequate commentary on a Biblical book, he is safe in turning to the *International Critical Commentary series* (Scribner's). For a condensed but satisfying help he is generally justified in purchasing the proper volume of the *New Century Bible* (Frowde) . Specific books belonging to other series will be mentioned below in the references for each study.

II - Reference Literature for Each Study

The first four references in each section will be to the appropriate pages of Sanders' "History of the Hebrews" (SHH), of Sanders and Kent's "Messages of the Earlier Prophets" (Mess EP), or "Messages of the Later Prophets" (Mess LP), of Kent's "Historical Bible" (Hist Bib), and of George Adam Smith's "Book of the Twelve" (Sm Twelve).

INTRODUCTION
SHH, 88-93, 107-109, 117, 136-139, 146-149; Mess EP, 3-19; Hist Bib I, 203; II, 38, 39, 74-76; III, 25-53; Sm Twelve I, 3-58.
CHAPTER I - AMOS
SHH, 149-153; Mess EP, 23-44; Hist Bib III, 53-79; Sm Twelve I, 61-207; Mitchell, "Amos, An Essay on Exegesis"; New Century, "Minor Prophets," I, 117-177; Smith, J. M, P., "Amos, Hosea, and Micah."
CHAPTER II - HOSEA AND ISAIAH
SHH, 153-161; Mess EP, 47-108; Hist Bib IH, 80102, 128-150; Sm Twelve I, 211-354; Whitehouse, New Century, "Isaiah I-XXXIX," passim.
CHAPTER III - MICAH AND ISAIAH
SHH, 162-170; Mess EP, 111-169; Hist Bib III, 150-181; Sm Twelve I, 357-438; Whitehouse; McFadyen, "Isaiah" (Bible for Home and School).
CHAPTER IV - ZEPHANIAH AND JEREMIAH
SHH, 173-182; Mess EP, 187-216; Hist Bib III, 192-218; Sm Twelve II, 3-74; Driver, New Century, "Jeremiah," passim.
CHAPTER V - NAHUM, JEREMIAH AND HABAKKUK
SHH, 183-192; Mess EP, 173-183, 219-262; Hist Bib III, 183-191, 236-269; Sm Twelve II, 77-159; Driver, New Century, "Jeremiah," passim.

CHAPTER VI - JEREMIAH AND EZEKIEL

SHH, 192-202; Mess EP, 265-296; Mess LP, 19-60; Hist Bib III, 269-307; Driver, New Century, "Jeremiah"; Davidson, Cambridge Bible "Ezekiel."

CHAPTER VII, EZEKIEL

SHH, 210-218; Mess LP, 72-128; Hist Bib IV, 8-23; Davidson, Cambridge Bible "Ezekiel"; McFadyen in Peake's "Commentary on the Bible," pp. 513-521.

CHAPTER VIII, ISAIAH 40-55

SHH, 219-228; Mess LP, 131-193; Hist Bib IV, 2334, 53-72, 95-104; Skinner, "Isaiah XI^-LXVI" (Cambridge Bible); G. A. Smith, "Isaiah," vol. II.

CHAPTER IX, HAGGAI AND ZECHARIAH

SHH, 229-241; Mess LP, 197-233; Hist Bib IV, 35-52; Sm Twelve II, 198-328; Driver, New Century, "Haggai and Zechariah," 1-8, 145-226.

CHAPTER X, ISAIAH 56-66, OBADIAH, MALACHI

SHH, 243-248; Mess LP, 237-285; Hist Bib IV, 6473; Sm Twelve II, 331-372; Driver, New Century, "Malachi," 285-329; Horton, New Century, "Obadiah," pp. 185-193.

CHAPTER XI, PROPHETIC-APOCALYPTIC VOICES

SHH, 275-276, 287; Mess LP 289-354; Hist Bib IV, 174-175, 141-142; Sm Twelve II, 375-541; Horton, New Century, "Joel," 79-114, "Jonah," 197-216; Driver, New Century, "Zechariah IX-XIV," 227-282.

III - Questions for Review

1. What is the best definition of a prophet?

2. What were the distinctive functions of a prophet among the Hebrews?

3. Trace the influences which led to the development of the prophetic order.

4. How may one explain the great influence and the numerical strength of the order.

5. Mention several notable prophets of the days before Amos. Why were Abraham and Moses called prophets?

6. What other portions of the Old Testament than the sixteen canonical prophetic books may properly be classified as prophetical and why?

7. Judging by no other criteria than quality and creativeness, which prophets would be ranked as major prophets?

8. Account for Isaiah's pre-eminence among the eighth century group of prophets.

9. Which of the four in the eighth century group brought forward the idea of deepest spiritual significance?

10. In what respects did the seventh century group of prophets reverse the declarations of their predecessors?

11. Name two great discoveries in religion which Jeremiah reached and through what process.

12. What three great services did Ezekiel render to the Babylonian exiles?

13. What supremely important religious idea did he formulate?

14. Who was the first prophet with a real missionary interpretation of Israel's relationship to the world?

15. Why did that note cease to influence the Jewish people after a little?

16. Justify the statement that Isaiah 40-55 is the highwater mark of prophetic thinking.

17. Distinguish between the prophetic and the apocalyptic view-points.

18. What prophets who lived prior to 400 B. C. showed traces of the apocalyptical temper?

19. What causes encouraged an emphasis on apocalypse in post-exilic times?

20. How did the prophets transform religion from a ritual into a mighty social force?

21. Draw out the whole range of essential prophetic thinking in such a series of statements as are found on page 27.

22. What justifies the reverent student in viewing the book of Jonah as a perfect parable about God rather than an episode in history?

23. What other examples may be given out of the Old Testament of the prophetically religious use of imaginative literature?

24. What is the basis for concluding that the whole book of Isaiah includes three clearly distinguishable periods of prophetic thinking?

25. What were the outstanding values of apocalyptical prophecy such as Isaiah 24-27?

26. What element in prophecy seems the most fundamental and characteristic?

27. Counting each distinct section of the prophetical writings, how many prophetic minds should we recognize in Hebrew and Jewish history?

28. How did Hebrew nationalism become a universalism of service?

29. Trace the growth and development of the Messianic idea.

30. What elements give enduring value to the prophetic writings?

31. What are the most important passages of Old Testament prophecy which describe the character of God?

32. What passages prepare the way for the thought of an intimate relationship with God or suggest such fellowship specifically?

33. What passages emphasize God's share in human history or in guiding individual destinies?

34. To what extent can you sum up each prophet's contributory thinking around one distinctive idea?

35. Which among the prophets had a clear social message?

36. Find four passages which would describe blameworthy social conditions of to-day.

37. What passages do you regard to be clearly Messianic?

38. What passages set forth the missionary program?

39. What is the prophetic utterance which seems nearest to New Testament revelation?

40. Which prophets contributed most to the thinking of Jesus?

IV - Subjects for Research and Class Discussion

If this book is used as a text-book by a class, the leader may find it profitable to devote the class session to the discussion of the important themes connected with each chapter. The following lists of topics for research and class discussion are suggested as bringing out some of the most essential themes.

INTRODUCTION AND CHAPTER I

1. The growth of the prophetic order. 2. The specific contribution of each prominent pre-literary prophet to his time. 3. The conditions which initiated literary prophecy. 4. The proof in the book of Amos (other than 7:14) that he was a farmer. 5. Similar proof that Assyria was to be the agency of Divine wrath.

CHAPTER II

1. The most probable explanation of God's revelation of Himself as abiding love to Hosea. 2. The distinctive personality of Amos, Hosea, and Isaiah. 3. The different way in which each was summoned to prophetic service. 4. The outstanding idea of God which dominated the thinking of each prophet. 5. How Isaiah supplemented the thinking of Amos and Hosea.

CHAPTER III

1. The position of Isaiah regarding alliances. 2. His reasons for believing that Jehovah would not permit Jerusalem to be destroyed. 3. Micah's personality as inferred from his prophecies. 4. The great religious ideas of the eighth-century prophets. 5. The limitations of their thinking.

CHAPTER IV

1. The effect of the persecutions of Manasseh's reign upon prophecy. 2. The occasion for the unmeasured denunciation of Jerusalem by Zephaniah. 3. A comparison of the personalities of Zephaniah and Jeremiah. 4. The spirit in which Jeremiah accepted prophetic service. 5. Their connection with Josiah's reformation.

CHAPTER V

1. The Biblical justification of Nahum's plea for vengeance. 2. The influence of the bitter ostracism of the early reign of Jehoiakim upon Jeremiah's spiritual convictions. 3. Habakkuk's philosophy of life. 4. The distinctive contribution of each prophet to the nation's distressing situation. 5. Jeremiah's explanation of the rapid transfers of political sovereignty.

CHAPTER VI

1. The wisdom of Jeremiah's advice to the Babylonian captives. 2. The comparison of Ezekiel's call to service with that of Isaiah. 3. The skill with which Ezekiel altered the conviction of the exiles concerning God's attitude toward Jerusalem.

4. The spiritual discoveries of Jeremiah. 5. A comparison of the seventh century prophetic thinking with that of the eighth century.

CHAPTER VII

1. A comparison of Jeremiah, Ezekiel and Isaiah as influential factors in Hebrew life. 2. The symbolism of Ezekiel. 3. Ezekiel the pastor. 4. Ezekiel's greatest prophecy. 5. His supreme contribution to religion.

CHAPTER VIII

1. The general effect of two generations of Babylonian exile upon the Hebrews. 2. The chapters of the book of Isaiah which belong to the exile or later. 3. The reasons prophetically given for the deliverance by Cyrus. 4. The program announced for the ransomed people. 5. How the high-water mark of religious thinking was reached.

CHAPTER IX

1. The contrast between the personalities and the methods of Haggai and Zechariah. 2. The four great themes of Haggai. 3. A comparison of Zechariah's thinking with that of Isaiah. 4. The symbolism of Zechariah. 5. The apocalyptical assertions of Haggai and Zechariah.

CHAPTER X

1. The noblest prophetic utterance of the fifth century. 2. The religious value of Obadiah. 3. Causes which led gradually to religious laxity in the Judean community. 4. Malachi's analysis of the situation and his remedy. 5. Fifth century prophetic thinking compared to that of the sixth century.

CHAPTER XI

1. Compare the attitude of Jonah to the world with that of Obadiah. 2. Joel's expectations regarding Jehovah's Day. 3. The comparison of prophecy and apocalypse. 4. The religious values of apocalypse. 5. The incompleteness of prophecy as an adequate interpretation of religion.

CHAPTER XII

1. The four prophets really entitled to rank as major prophets. 2. The six groups under which all prophets may be classified. 3. The essential teaching of each prophet about God. 4. The inevitable climax of Hebrew-Jewish religious thinking in a missionary program. 5. The causes which contributed to retire this program to the background of Jewish thought.